North
of Caution

North of Caution

A journey through the
conservation economy
on the northwest coast
of British Columbia

ecotrust CANADA

Ecotrust Canada is a private, nonprofit organization promoting the emergence of a conservation economy in the coastal temperate rain forests of British Columbia. Ecotrust Canada works with conservation entrepreneurs, local communities, First Nations, all levels of government, scientists, industry, and fellow conservationists. We are agents of change, catalysts in the ongoing search for true protection and sustainability of British Columbia's unmatched natural legacy.

A conservation economy sustains itself on "principled income" earned from activities and practices that restore rather than deplete natural capital. We envision a region in which the economy results in social and ecological improvements rather than degradation.

Ecotrust Canada was founded in Vancouver in 1994 and has offices based in Vancouver and Ucluelet. Ecotrust Canada's affiliates include Ecotrust in Portland, Oregon and ShoreBank Pacific and Shorebank Enterprise Pacific in Ilwaco, Washington.

Ecotrust Canada
202 – 1226 Hamilton Street
Vancouver, BC V6B 2S8
Tel: 604.682.4141
Fax: 604.682.1944
Website: www.ecotrustcan.org

NATIONAL LIBRARY OF CANADA CATALOGUING IN PUBLICATION DATA
Main entry under title:
North of Caution

ISBN 1-896866-03-4

1. Pacific Coast (B.C.) 2. Conservation of natural resources--British Columbia--Pacific Coast. 3. Sustainable development--British Columbia--Pacific Coast. 4. Indians of North America--British Columbia--Pacific Coast. I. Gill, Ian, 1955- II. Ecotrust Canada.
   HC117.B8N67 2001 333.7'2'097111 C2001-911049-9

Price: $22.00
Additional copies of this publication may be purchased through Ecotrust Canada.

Top left image: "The Smart One" carved by Dempsey Bob: a powerful mask created from memories of his own Tlingit oral history . PHOTO BY ROMAN SKOTNICKI
Centre scenic image: Galsgiyst, a sacred Nisga's site in Observatory Inlet at the mouth of the Nass River, the northern most reaches of the study area for this book. PHOTO BY GARY FIEGEHEN.

Book design by Sage Design, Vancouver, BC.

Printed on NuLife Opaque paper containing 30% post consumer waste and 70% Elemental Chlorine-Free Virgin Fibre by Western Printers & Lithographers, Burnaby, BC.

Contents

Canada's Forgotten Coast

By Ian Gill

NORTH OF CAUTION, CAPE CAUTION THAT IS, THERE LIES A BEGUILING REGION WHERE THE promise of a conservation economy is within reach. Different people call it different things. Canada's Forgotten Coast. The Great Bear Rain Forest. The Central Coast. The Inside Passage. Land of the Spirit Bear. The Mid-Coast. British Columbia's Hidden Heart. The Northwest Coast. Home.

There are something like eight million acres of coastal temperate rainforests in this region. These forests exist where the land meets the sea, and are among the most complex and diverse ecosystems on Earth. In prime sites, the biomass in these temperate rain forests is four times as great as any comparable area in the tropics.

That these forests are increasingly rare and threatened is hardly news. That eight million acres outside of parks saw out the 20th century largely intact is so remarkable as to be almost unbelievable.

North of Caution, it is still possible to find whole watersheds – tens of thousands of acres at a time – that are unlogged and largely unaltered by man. Millions of acres in all, home to grizzly, black and Kermode (white) bears, home to the salmon that feed the bears and provide nutrients to the streams and the soil, home to wolves and eagles and, of course, to huge hemlock and spruce and cedar trees.

Various campaigns are afoot to "save" these forests. People are being urged to "discover" these supposedly "forgotten" lands. But what is most easily forgotten – what was forgotten for most of the 20th century by governments and industry and, yes, even environmentalists – is that this coast isn't forgotten at all. It may be home to all manner of diverse creatures and complex biological relationships, but it is also home to diverse cultures and complex societies of *people*.

Canada's Forgotten Coast has in fact been home, for around 10,000 years, to the Heiltsuk and the Tsimshian and the Haisla and the Kitasoo-Xaixais and the Owekeeno and the Kwakiutl and the Nuxalk, to name a few. These are who Canadians refer to as their *First* Nations, though for 100 years and more they have been last in line for the social and economic benefits that have flowed from B.C.'s abundant resources.

Canada's Forgotten Coast has never been forgotten by First Nations. It is remembered through oral histories, and through some of the greatest and most enduring works of art in the world. Western red cedar began to dominate these forests about 3,000 BC, around the same time that, in the archaeological record, specialized tools emerged on the coast. These tools were used to hew planks for imposing longhouses and ocean-going dugout canoes. Cedar was used to make armour and weapons. It was steamed into bentwood boxes for storing food, and the fibre from its inner bark was

woven into clothing. It was carved into majestic totem poles, and into masks whose almost Gothic power still sends a shiver down all but the most rigid spine.

As for salmon, it was and is the mainstay of the First People's diet. Salmon arrived at the close of the last Ice Age and colonized the glacier-fed streams. People in turn colonized the rivermouths and other strategic fishing sites. A fishing village that was established at Namu is thought to be one of the first fishing villages anywhere on Earth. Marvellous technologies emerged, and especially efficient were traps, weirs and dams. Of the two dozen ancestral villages recorded in the oral traditions of the Nuxalk people alone, all were associated with a fish trap. One estimate has it that "pre-contact" tribal fisheries hauled in 127 million pounds of salmon annually – and these fisheries were sustainable. In addition to salmon, First Nations relied heavily on herring, shellfish, and marine plants like seaweed and kelp. Studies have shown that, historically, 90 per cent of the protein in people's diets was marine-derived.

And then, contact. White people, and white people's diseases, in particular smallpox. It arrived at about the same time as the first commercial canneries. Whole communities were wiped out. Native villages fell silent, while along the coast new villages sprung up: cannery villages. By the 1920s, there were more than 70 canneries operating on the B.C. coast, except the modern-day harvest of salmon and other marine species was unsustainable and the canning industry collapsed and these villages, too, fell silent.

And now it's the turn of the forests. Canada's Forgotten Coast is largely unroaded. Easier access to forest lands on Vancouver Island, and further north and south on the mainland, left a sort of island of forest lands largely untouched on the central coast – till now.

Now, the harvest of these last stands is underway in earnest. It's hard to be precise about how much is being logged, because of the confusion of jurisdictions and entitlements and licences –

The Kitlope Valley, traditional territory of the Haisla First Nation. This stunningly beautiful area has remained untouched by commercial logging.
DYLAN SIMONDS

because of the typical fog that descends when statistics blow in along the coast. But a rough estimate is that logging on the central coast currently stands at about 1 million cubic metres a year, which is twice the level even the Forest Service estimates is sustainable.

That's the equivalent of 1 million telephone poles. These go out mostly on barges, which float right by native villages, an unintentional taunt to people who have watched for over a century while their culture and the marine resources have been stripped from them.

Except in recent years, two things have changed.

First, most of B.C.'s First Nations are now involved in negotiating treaties for their land, which was never legally ceded to the "Crown." Suddenly, emboldened by a string of Supreme Court decisions in their favour, native people are staking a claim to their territories and the resources in them. It might be 100 years late, but native governments are now being taken seriously. Hearteningly, there is a natural conservation ethic among many native people, and the prospects for responsible stewardship of resources are good.

Second, there is a baby boom on native reserves, or a "population time bomb" as it has been described. In Canada, as in most "first world" economies, the general population is getting older. The one anomaly is on native reserves, where on average more than half the population is under 25. What this means is that First Nations are undergoing a spirited revival after a century of repression, depression and marginalization. What it also means is that there will be more, not fewer people, looking for meaningful work, and a way to sustain their growing communities.

For the environmental movement – as for industry, governments and indeed native people themselves – this is new and complex terrain. Wilderness campaigns that don't accommodate people will fail. The challenge on Canada's Forgotten Coast is not to stop logging or fishing, but to *start* an economy that grows within the ecological limits of the region's resources, and builds social equity,

Shaman's rattle made of cedar. Cedar had many uses, including totem poles, clothing, dishes and ceremonial artifacts.
GARY FIEGEHEN

especially for historically deprived native people. At Ecotrust Canada, we call that a conservation economy. Our book, *North of Caution*, is offered here not as a prescription, but as a navigational device to enable us all to steer towards a conservation economy. In preparing this book, we have learned much more than we could ever presume to teach. So we present what we have learned along the way in order that others might share our journey, and come to appreciate the enormous opportunities that await people North of Caution.

For us, the Great *People* Rain Forest includes bears, and salmon, and trees, but it succeeds only if we preserve not just trees, but options for people to live lives of dignity and prosperity, where culture flourishes and new myths and a new economy emerge from the mists of possibly the most spectacular wild place left on Earth.

Our book [is] offered here not as a prescription, but as a navigational device to enable us all to steer towards a conservation economy

Chapter	# The Speaker's Post
1	*By Richard Manning*

IN HER BOOK *CEDAR*, AN ACCOUNT OF THE USES OF WOOD IN NATIVE PACIFIC COASTAL CULTURE, Hilary Stewart reports that carvings played a key role in greeting honoured guests. Welcoming you here as a reader is part of the business of this introductory essay. This book is about wood, masks, culture, trade and the practices that organize northern coastal life, so it is useful for a moment to consider her information:

"As a welcoming gesture to important guests arriving by canoe for a feast or potlatch, a large carved figure of a human was placed at the edge of the beach, facing out to sea. Part of the greeting ceremonies was the speaker's post, a carved ancestral figure with an open perforated mouth; the officially appointed speaker stood behind it to announce the names of guests as though the ancestor himself was receiving the visitors."

It is with a particular sense of need that I call on this idea here at the outset, in the greeting. A proper welcome requires the anonymity of a mask. I know so little about the northwest coast of British Columbia, having only wandered it off and on for a year or so now. I've only begun to peel back some of the layers on the information that has accreted among the various cultures – human and otherwise, native and otherwise – that inhabit here. Yet even this little bit of wandering counsels the same sense of humility that caused the people who knew the northwest coast best to stand behind a mask when speaking for the whole community. None of us ever knows it sufficiently to speak for the whole. In many ways, that is the spirit that is to govern much of what follows in these pages. Behind the mask that is the cover of this book, there stands a small community of writers and wanderers, each of whom has threaded a particular meandering course through the turns of coastal life.

The account of a region cannot rest simply on a bare description of the place, but it can start there. Simply, we speak herein of a region of the extreme western edge of

Alver Tait, of the Nisga'a First Nation, carving the Bear Den Pole. Erected in 1992 in Canyon City (Gitwinksihlky) on the Nass River, it was the first pole erected in Nisga'a territory in more than 100 years. GARY FIEGEHEN

North America that people in and nearby know as the northwest coast. It is the strip of temperate rain forest, the weaving fjords, the islands of land and not land that lie between the Pacific proper on the west and the coastal ranges of mountains that wall British Columbia's Interior. It is that portion of B.C. north of Cape Caution, and maybe that says enough to orient the maritime sensibility of the place. Maybe living beyond caution has something to do with successfully inhabiting the place, but for now we will hang with the straight geographical facts of the matter (see map 1.1).

The region's west edge holds the island systems of Haida Gwaii or the Queen Charlotte Islands, mostly water, but the balance shifts as sea fades to mainland coast, not a sharp line like most coasts, but a meander that extends far to the Interior, as far as Smithers, the eastern gateway to the Skeena and Bulkley Rivers. It includes all of the ground and water between the Nass and Bella Coola Rivers, some 500 kilometres bounded by the coastal communities of Port Simpson in the north and Namu in the south. The region is approximately double the size of Vancouver Island, covering some 125,000 square kilometres of land, 200,000 when the marinescape is included. Of the 72,000 people resident there, 25 per cent are aboriginal (see map 1.3). This is a rural, northern, and marine oriented region, considered a resource hinterland by the south and thought of as home among its diversified and scattered population.

A book can begin to describe a people by examining a snapshot of their economy, one small measure of what they do. Those living further south used to thinking of this sparsely settled place (2 per cent of B.C.'s total population) as a resource hinterland are in part right. As of 1996, about 10.5 per cent of the wage earners worked in fishing and trapping or forestry, more than double the percentage for the province as a whole. Behind these statistics stand others typical of resource hinterlands worldwide: unemployment runs to 15 per cent, close to double the province's rate overall. There are more jobs elsewhere, but something about the place makes its people reticent to go elsewhere.

Yet the static snapshot of statistics drawn from 1996 masks something more that is no secret to residents of the place. Employment in primary industries like logging and fishing is falling. Service sector jobs are on the rise. The region is in a state of flux and will be for some time to come. Another statistic promises this: 26 per cent of the total population is less than age 14, compared to 19.7 per cent for B.C. as a whole. The place is young, it is changing and much of life here is boxed by the coming to grips with those two elements. Unease over an uncertain future lands on children.

Whatever the future, it's best to know at the outset that the place was shaped by a tough past, also not news to its people. Even before most whites came, the government was getting a grip on the character of northwest coast residents, a notion that echoes in a warning laid out to would-be settlers in 1902:

"It is not desirable, either in the interest of the Province or the proposed Bulkley Colony itself, that the development of enterprise should be hampered by men and women who are unused by experience to the trials of pioneer life, unfitted by training to take up the work of actual farm labour, and unable by physical endurance to withstand the hard labour involved. It must be understood that settlers who go in there will, for some time, be wholly isolated, and that for three years at least their property will be unproductive. The prospects for success are very good…but the way to success is long and hard, and without pluck, untiring industry, intelligent effort, self-reliance, physical endurance, and some capital to back up these qualities, disappointment and failure are sure to result. Those who are not prepared to accept the situation as stated and stick with it, had better remain where they are."

The region is approximately double the size of Vancouver Island, covering some 125,000 square kilometres of land, 200,000 when the marinescape is included. Of the 72,000 people resident there, 25 per cent are aboriginal

These are notions now deeply encoded in a regional psyche, so much so that quoting them is redundant. Less so a modern day quote from the *Prince Rupert Daily News* that at first seems to ring in opposition to the above:

"In the past, all that northwest coast people had to do to make a living was cut a few trees or catch what swam past or work in related support services. The recent dramatic changes in fishing, public perception about resource use and mis-use, logging markets and technology means we can no longer rely on what we have done in the past to sustain us in the future. That may not be the worst message in the world."

Opposition? The more we consider it, not really. That's the case that eventually will emerge: that the two quotes agree more than not.

This introduction needs the cover of a speaker's post because what follows is a compilation of writings by several writers. On one level, this book is simply a straightforward look at the region's culture and economy by sector. Terry Glavin, a veteran journalist, begins this journey with an examination of fishing, but because fishing is so intimately linked to the life of this place, what unfolds is a sort of history, even a deep history, all wrapping around a place called Namu. Ben Parfitt, long-time timber writer, took on forestry, but echoes many of the themes teased out by Glavin. Part of this history draws on ancient, almost forgotten traditions of the region's more than 25 First Nations communities, where a cultural rebirth is underway. This is described by the province's most experienced author on the subject, Alex Rose (see map 1.2). Finally, three authors – Pauline Waterfall, Doug Hopwood, and Ian Gill – join forces to describe how culture and modern science are combining in Heiltsuk territory as First Nations work to regain control of the resources that are rightfully theirs.

We end finally with a small story, one set in traditional conservation, the saving of the Kitlope Valley from logging and for sustaining the Haisla people. The story is told by Ian Gill, who works with the conservation group Ecotrust which aided the Haisla Nation in saving the valley. On its surface, the Kitlope's story seems a straightforward lesson in conservation, but seen in the light of everything that has come before, its story is emblematic of the whole.

We argue herein not for separation of nature from economy, but for sustaining natural productivity to sustain our communities' lives.

Mathieson Channel, north of Bella Bella. The waters of the B.C. coast weave through numerous islands, rocky outcroppings, sandy beaches and majestic fjords.
DAVE NUNUK

All this is to say this book is going to cover some ground, both physically and intellectually. You guests should know at the outset, however, that there was a charge to each of us to assemble something more than the laundry list of facts, the snippets and comings and goings that are the detail of history. Something else was at work.

◎ ◎ ◎

A mask carver when complimented on his work often will defer, saying simply that he did not create the mask. That the lines of the mask were in the tree. He just saw it there and let it out.

In the same sense, there can be no design laid out for a northwest coast future. That's not our purpose here, to behave as social engineers and to generalize what we have learned to a blueprint, a design, an agenda. The lines of the northwest coast's future will not be drawn by writers. If there is a theme to emerge from the history detailed herein, it is that those who have attempted to impose a preconceived notion or agenda on this landscape have failed. The place will dictate its own design. The lines of this plan are already in the tree. We can muck it up by failing to correctly read the lines or we can do it right. The residents, the people, are not mere spectators in all of this. It is our job to try to read the lines and see where we are

headed, to learn what we must do to become successful inhabitants of this powerful landscape. This book is a modest attempt at reading a few of the more straightforward lines.

My faith in the strength of these lines was greatly bolstered in the gathering of the detail of the book. For instance, I can tell you there was no design at the outset among the various writers to deal with or say a thing about native art and carving; quite the opposite, we focused on economy. Yet some of us came back to art and carving. In retrospect, it's difficult to imagine how it could be any other way. Art, organic art, indigenous art, aboriginal art, these are expressions of the spirit of the place. When we seek and reach to explain ourselves, to fully comprehend, then we naturally reach to art. Why should this book be any different? In our case, examination of carving is particularly appropriate. There is more to this than the fact that the northwest coast has supported carvers as opposed to, say, weavers or potters or painters, for most of the 10 millennia or so it has been inhabited by humans. This is a place of trees, and because there is wood here, there should be carvers just as there should be loggers.

Yet there is a deeper layer to this connection. Who among us has not counted the rings of a tree, the annular rings, which is to say, a record of the years? Their spacing, their warps and weaves, record the information of the place across time. Wet, warm years space wide rings, storms and catastrophe print in whorls, fire scars, disease stunts. In cross section, these lines become what a woodworker knows as grain, and it is the grain that informs the carver's chisel as to where to find the mask. The mask reads the history of the place in a literal sense. The bare physical, fundamental fact of the matter is in the end the mask.

There is something even more fundamental about this facet of our work. Consider, as you will more deeply in reading Parfitt's piece on logging, that the dominant use now of the region's trees is pulpwood. He will lay out a clear case that this represents a squandering of the region's resource in

Traditional carving tools. Many First Nations of B.C.'s north coast have maintained the carving methods created by their ancestors more than 10,000 years ago.
GARY FIEGEHEN

that pulp squeezes the fewest jobs per tree of any of the possible uses of wood. This unveils first the disorganizing enigma of the place, that increasing economic activity and increasing the volume of wood cut has *decreased* economic well-being of its inhabitants. Parfitt contrasts pulping with the work of a Prince Rupert man who makes Sitka spruce and western red cedar into guitar tops. This man says in doing so he can provide a living for three to five families from about five trees per year. Clearly, the value of these guitar tops comes from the grain of the wood, a particular interplay of natural forces that causes the top to resonate harmoniously. Its value is information, both as nature laid out its record in the tree and in the hands of the people who read that information to bring out its aesthetic and economic value.

Contrast this now with pulping, which takes all trees, regardless of history or inherent abilities, and reduces them by grinding them to the lowest common denominator. In this way, the potential for everlasting song becomes toilet paper.

Something similar is at work in the salmon fishery, and has been at work for more than a century. Some of the highest quality protein on the planet is reduced to canned fish, another sort of lowest common denominator, all so that it will ship to the universal and indiscriminate global market. In Glavin's work on fisheries, we will encounter a couple of examples of how enterprising people of the coast have found a way to circumvent this process, and by respecting the high quality of native wild salmon have been able to command the premium price that the region's bounty deserves. In the end, this is respect for information. Examples like these foreshadow a theme that will organize this work, a series of themes spun around the model of industrialism. The region was colonized and developed by Europeans largely coincident with the industrial revolution. It is not enough to say that machines – our tools – arrived in this region to carry out our work. The arrival of these tools is significant, and the book shall visit places that were once centres of this industrial penetration, now great rusting heaps

Preserved Nisga'a traditional foods. Traditional knowledge about foods was passed from one generation to the next.
GARY FIEGEHEN

of gutted-out canneries and old sawmills closing. These rusting heaps are now a part of the archaeological record of the place. Yet the industrial model was a great deal more than the physical invasion by these machines. It was a mode of thought in which the landscape was made to behave like a machine. The forest and streams became factories valued only for single outputs: trees and fish. Nature was expected to produce them with all the predictability and regularity of a well-oiled assembly line.

The piles of machinery lie rusting because the industrial age is passing. It is not this book's job to argue for its end; it is ending of its own accord. Our job now lies more in groping for a system of production and system of ideas to replace it. There is already a deep understanding among the people of this place that the place is more than a unit of production. It is a way of life. With the rest of the world, the northwest coast is moving to a post-industrial phase. It is more our job here to explain what is necessary to effectively weather that transition. The transition is complex, but if we could reduce it to a single idea, it is that industrialism erred in ignoring the complex information of the place.

... the book shall visit places that were once centres of this industrial penetration, now great rusting heaps of gutted-out canneries and old sawmills closing

It converted the region's life to exported wealth, just as asset strippers raid the pension funds and capital of the companies on which they prey. We argue for converting respect for the life of the place into rich lives for its inhabitants. Industrialism made pulp when it should have read the grain. If we are to succeed as inhabitants it will be by recovering information: knowledge of the habits of salmon, the layers of meaning of the land, the complexities of genetics; the wisdom of stories, command of craft, sure hands on chisel, net and keyboard. As I have said, it helps to approach this idea through art.

My years as a journalist have taught me that the toughest interviews are of people who work well with their hands. It is not that they lack answers to my questions; the same experience has taught me they often have far more resonant thoughts than the usual stable of talking heads and pundits that dominate column inches and news hour segments these days. It is more that they are used to expressing their best thoughts in their work. How does one catch this knowledge in a sentence or two?

'There's something about all of this rusted machinery and piles and docks falling apart and all these boats crumbling that's pretty inspiring'

One cold and rainy evening, as it can only be cold and rainy on a Prince Rupert winter's evening, I paced about Henry Green's little carving shed in the middle of town watching him work and trying to get him to say what his work so obviously said. Henry is a Tsimshian carver and he works both in metals and wood. He carves poles.

Some sentences come easily to him, especially when it's a good story and the joke is on him, as was his yarn about being invited to visit Switzerland and climbing off a plane exhausted and jet-lagged to meet a few people. He walked through a door to the meeting to find he faced an auditorium full of people, not to mention TV cameras, that had assembled to hear someone who Switzerland regarded as a great artist.

Ask him where his art comes from, or how he learned it, and the answers are less direct. There is some talk of relatives and things he learned from this one and that and from some books he picked up along the way. Then he's quiet for a while as the rain pounds the shop's little windows and the glow of heat mixes with the smell of cedar chips to hold the chill at bay. He concentrates especially as he is sharpening gouges, knives and adz, the biggest part of his work he tells me. The trick of carving is in the quality of the edge on one's tools.

The pole he is carving is maybe three metres tall, but resting on its back, a solid block of cedar. Each gentle whack of the hand-built adz in Green's hand sends it to thumping like a drum. Faces of creatures emerge. This pole is already sold to a gallery in Portland, Oregon and will be flown later in the winter to a show in Arizona.

The creatures flow from the wood, but also from each other. Transformation is at the core of native art. It often examines how one creature becomes another or contains another, and to Green that is the story. "That's the beauty of art. It speaks directly to your mythological mind," Green said. "It's about transition. When you are in a transition period, you give up your illusions and delusions."

Amy Heustis once created her art in a place that seems stripped of its illusions. Like this book will do, she asked questions of the place and found the answers eventually led her to an abandoned cannery, the old North Pacific Cannery twenty minutes' drive up the Skeena River from Prince Rupert. She lived in one of the little frame houses in the row at the cannery's edge where the supervisors once lived. Her studio was at the edge of an old net loft. Each day she walked to work threading a path through the silent skeletons of cannery machinery. While living there, Amy said of the cannery. "It's crumbling. I really like to live by the water. That's one reason, I'm here, but this is crumbling. It's in ruins. There's something about all of this rusted machinery and piles and docks falling apart and all these boats crumbling that's pretty inspiring," she said. "There's a creative energy to this place."

Heustis came to the cannery with an outsider's awe of the place's power. She came to Rupert after formal art training in Montreal. Although a cannery at first can seem an odd window into a place's artistic tradition, Heustis quickly learned this was not so. The northwest coast has a vital and growing network of respected native artists. A quick check of their biographies found many directly linked to canneries, especially the Northern Pacific Cannery. As the region's major employers, the canneries drew together families from throughout the region, and it was at these gatherings that vital connections were made. Economic centres are cultural centres, and they foster vibrant art.

There is nothing new in this phenomenon. The artists working today tend to give salmon a revered spot in their work because they understand it was the bounty of the salmon that allowed a society to give artists their leisure to work. But there is a deeper connection, a weave between life, life's work and the forces that hold it together, that the fisher's hand and artist's hand is driven by the same power.

The connection remains powerful enough that it steered Heustis from painting and into a unique community project. In 1998 a group of Rupert people worked together to weave a traditional native salmon net built of nettle fibres. She said part of her attraction to the project came from working in a netloft, from speaking with visitors to the loft who remember hanging nets there as children, from realizing how the community's life stories are bound up in fishing and from realizing that the weaving of a good net is art.

"When people first were here, they didn't have a net," she said. A spirit came and showed them how to make a net. It gave them technology so they would have time to do things like art. Now the net has caught too many fish. If people go back and

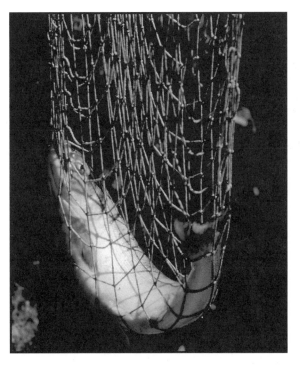

Creativity and practicality combined in many native tools. Fishing nets were traditionally made from stinging nettles, with floats made from hand carved pieces of wood in the shape of a fish. GARY FIEGEHEN

learn how to make a net, they touch that story. They ponder what has happened. I think it will change their thinking."

Dempsey Bob is a renowned carver, a world class artist who lives in a simple frame house in Prince Rupert. His basement is a clutter of tools and mockups; his kitchen table covered in books of sketches that begin each of his carvings, but from the clutter emerges the raw force of lines and the strength of form that makes each of Bob's carved faces stand alive as distinct and compelling characters. Like Henry Green's work, Bob's walks the line between animal and human, then blends the line allowing form to transform to form melding humanity into the broader collection of life that contains it.

The magic of this works especially well if one considers perspective. He shows me a wolf that has a man's face on its forehead. Both stare straight ahead and neither can see the other; they are outside of each other's field of vision.

A spirit came and showed them how to make a net. It gave them technology so they would have time to do things like art

"The Smart One," a powerful character from Tlingit lore. Mask carved by Dempsey Bob.
ROMAN SKOTNICKI

He says art is vision. "You don't know that you know it, but it's all there," he said. "There's no life without vision. Without vision, you're just there."

He says an artist is a creator, that his job involves far more than simply a recreation of the past, a copying of tradition, but in the same way, it is his job to be attentive to the stories that made his Tahltan-Tlingit culture, that his work must grow from the foundation of this place-based tradition. "If you innovate from nothing, it's still nothing," he said. "My grandmother says our art is who we are. It's what we are. It's in our things. It's in our blankets. It's in our masks. It's in our bracelets. It's in our drums," he said. "I believe you can't separate the people from the land from the culture. That's what art is."

All of these ideas are foundation for the story of the Smart One, a mask Bob carved and whose image appears on the cover of this book. Among the pantheon of powerful faces that have flowed from his hands, the Smart One still stands out: broad, black arched eyebrows, deep knowing, almost smug eyes and fat red lips set in a grin that is not a grin. He is his own man, and this is how Bob speaks of him.

The Smart One is a character Bob had heard about only vaguely in stories, one who knew all the stories, all of the information. Because of this, he became a figure of great power. But somehow or another he himself became lost in the general loss of story among the Tlingit. Bob believed he should be resurrected and set out to carve him.

But then the mask seemed to carve itself, or at least that's how Bob tells it, that during the working he had the unsettling experience of watching himself carve from a distance, like he was outside of his body looking down into his studio. Simply, it scared him, but he stayed in the process to watch the mask become what it wanted to be. "He turned out better than I ever thought. It was an honour just to be a part of him."

I mean to suggest by retelling this story that Dempsey Bob was given a face for our times, not just for the Tlingit or natives, but for all of the people of the coast. I am not writing a story about art now, but about the life and economy of the northwest coast. The Smart One emerges. This is the face I wish to place on the stories that follow.

REFERENCES

Colpits, H. November, 3, 1997. *Prince Rupert Daily News.*

Statistics Canada, Census of Population and Housing. 1996. "1996 Census Profile of British Columbia's Census Subdivisions (CSD) – Profile of Central Coast Regional District." Produced by BC Stats.

Stewart, H. 1984. "*Cedar: tree of life to the Northwest Coast Indians.*" Douglas & McIntyre Ltd. Vancouver, BC. 192p.

MAP 1.1 North of Caution locator map

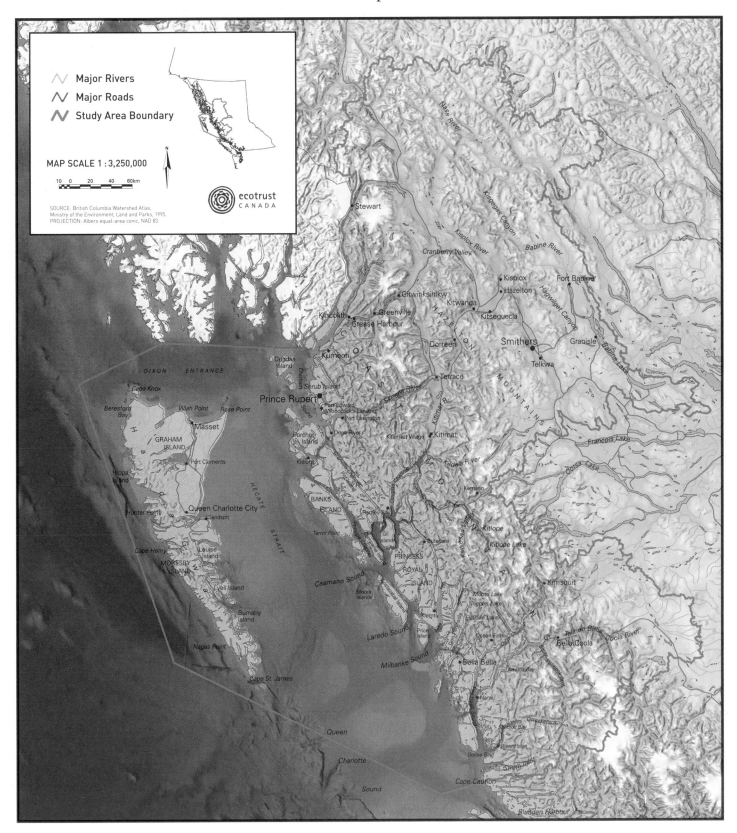

Major Rivers

Major Roads

Study Area Boundary

MAP SCALE 1 : 3,250,000

10 0 20 40 60km

N

ecotrust
CANADA

SOURCE: British Columbia Watershed Atlas,
Ministry of the Environment, Land and Parks, 1995.
PROJECTION: Albers equal-area conic, NAD 83.

MAP 1.2 Statement of Intent boundaries

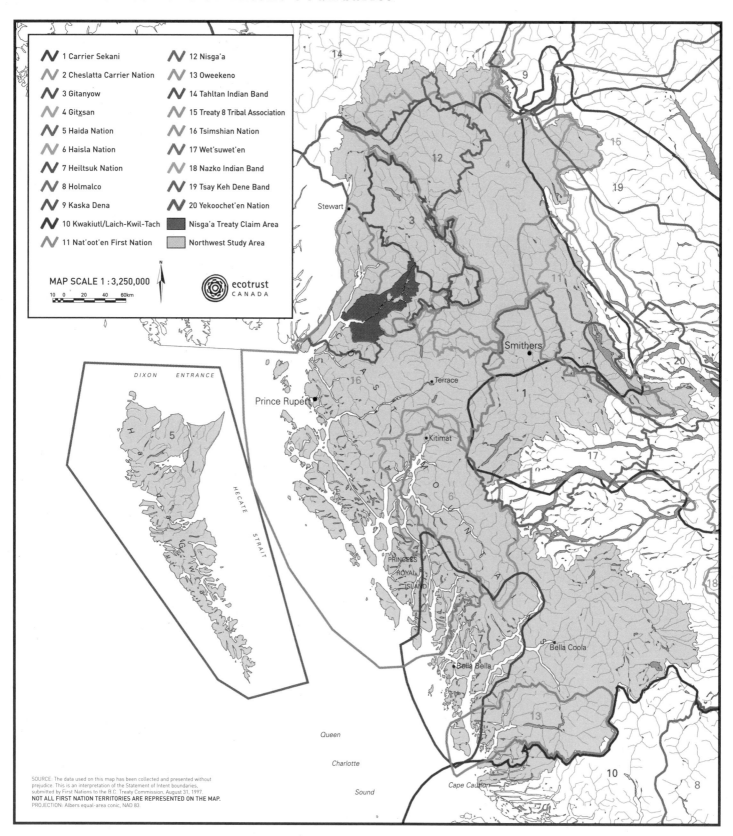

MAP SCALE 1 : 3,250,000

10 0   20   40   60km

N

ecotrust
C A N A D A

1 Carrier Sekani
2 Cheslatta Carrier Nation
3 Gitanyow
4 Gitxsan
5 Haida Nation
6 Haisla Nation
7 Heiltsuk Nation
8 Holmalco
9 Kaska Dena
10 Kwakiutl/Laich-Kwil-Tach
11 Nat'oot'en First Nation

12 Nisga'a
13 Oweekeno
14 Tahltan Indian Band
15 Treaty 8 Tribal Association
16 Tsimshian Nation
17 Wet'suwet'en
18 Nazko Indian Band
19 Tsay Keh Dene Band
20 Yekoochet'en Nation

Nisga'a Treaty Claim Area

Northwest Study Area

DIXON ENTRANCE

HECATE STRAIT

Stewart

Smithers

Terrace

Prince Rupert

Kitimat

PRINCESS ROYAL ISLAND

Bella Coola

Bella Bella

Queen Charlotte Sound

Cape Caution

SOURCE: The data used on this map has been collected and presented without
prejudice. This is an interpretation of the Statement of Intent boundaries,
submitted by First Nations to the B.C. Treaty Commission, August 31, 1997.
NOT ALL FIRST NATION TERRITORIES ARE REPRESENTED ON THE MAP.
PROJECTION: Albers equal-area conic, NAD 83.

MAP 1.3 Population

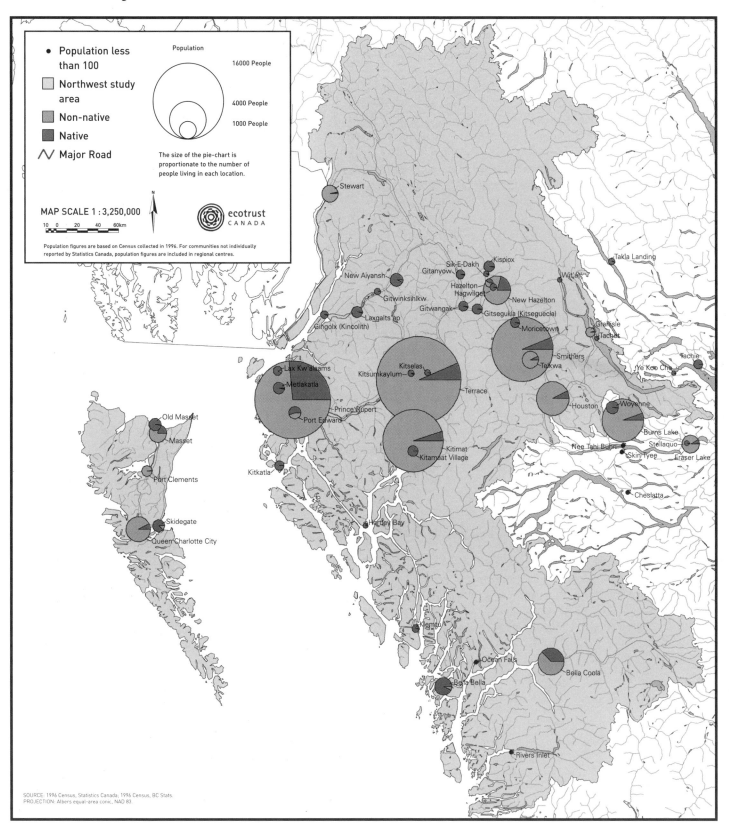

Population less than 100

Northwest study area

Non-native

Native

Major Road

Population

16000 People

4000 People

1000 People

The size of the pie-chart is proportionate to the number of people living in each location.

MAP SCALE 1 : 3,250,000

10 0   20   40   60km

ecotrust CANADA

Population figures are based on Census collected in 1996. For communities not individually reported by Statistics Canada, population figures are included in regional centres.

Stewart

Sik-E-Dakh   Kispiox

Gitanyow

New Aiyansh

Gitwinksihlkw

Hazelton   Wit'at

Hagwilget

New Hazelton

Laxgalts'ap   Gitwangak

Gitsegukla (Kitseguecla)

Gingolx (Kincolith)

Moricetown   Grahisle

Tachet

Smithers   Tachie

Kitselas   Telkwa   Ye Koo Che

Kitsumkaylum

Lax Kw'alaams   Terrace   Woyenne

Metlakatla   Houston   Burns Lake

Old Masset   Prince Rupert   Stellaquo

Masset   Port Edward   Nee Tahi Buhn   Fraser Lake

Kitimat   Skin Tyee

Kitamaat Village

Port Clements   Kitkatla   Cheslatta

Skidegate

Queen Charlotte City

Takla Landing

Hartley Bay

Klemtu

Ocean Falls   Bella Coola

Bella Bella

Rivers Inlet

SOURCE: 1996 Census, Statistics Canada; 1996 Census, BC Stats.
PROJECTION: Albers equal-area conic, NAD 83.

<table>
<tr><td>Chapter</td><td># The Waters</td></tr>
<tr><td>2</td><td>*By Terry Glavin*</td></tr>
</table>

Chapter	# The Waters
2	*By Terry Glavin*

WE WERE IN A CAVERNOUS ROOM, HOLLOW AND PITCH DARK, WITH THE SOUND OF WATER DRIP-ping somewhere. We had come 70 sea miles north of the northern tip of Vancouver Island, about half way up Fitzhugh Sound, to a cedar-shrouded cove that takes its name from the Heiltsuk word Na'wamu, which translates roughly as "everything is close by." There had been a Heiltsuk village here once, and its name was Mah'was, which means, roughly, "loading place." But, as for the echoing chamber where we stood, which was being slowly entombed by the rain forest, gradually collapsing into the salal and bracken fern and brambles, and already half-devoured, it was not at all clear what the place was, exactly. There were what appeared to be church pews strewn around, but it couldn't have been a chapel, because it was just down a dimly-lit corri-dor from the sloping maplewood floors of what had once been a basketball court. It took a few minutes to adjust to the dark, but then I could make out just enough to see where we were. This was the bowling alley.

What had happened here was something that had lasted almost a century. Along the jagged and labyrinthine coast north of Cape Caution, known by 19th century coastal traders as The Jungles, the industrial revolution arrived with the likes of Robert Draney, a soft-spoken blacksmith who stepped ashore near here in 1893 and said, yes, this looks like a proper place. From that day, Na'wamu became Namu, and the harbour came alive with the noise of steam donkeys, a sawmill, gas engines, and clanking can-nery machines. In the mere 100 or so sea miles between Vancouver Island's northern capes and Bella Bella, tucked away inside the maze of channels and inlets, there were once 23 cannery towns like Namu (see map 2.2). There were Quashela and Kildala and Wannock. There was McTavish, Strathcona and Goose Bay. North of Namu, there were another 58 cannery towns, all the way to the Nass. The Union Steamships line

Commercial Haida fishing boat at Skidegate, Haida Gwaii, 1947. After providing steady sustenance for millennia, fish stocks have recently declined, leaving First Nations youth facing a changing economy. BC ARCHIVES, # I-22217

had more than 20 regular ports of call. Namu was more or less in the middle of it all, just about half way between the Nass and the Fraser.

At the end of the 20th century, the Namu Hilton was hollow and forlorn. There was what was left of the grandly named Edgewater, all 68 suites of it, with its sloping floors, dripping roof and barricaded entrance. Downtown, so to speak, bars covered the windows of the Canada Post station (Namu, V0T 1N0). A steel door, with its door handle shaped like a beer mug, was locked tight on the liquor store. The laundromat was crumbling, and the machine shop, grocery store, and welding shop were silent. Through the windows of the barbershop, scrawled on a blackboard: Cuts, $15. Colours, $35. Perms, $40. Highlights, $35. Kids, $8, for all appearances like everybody just picked up one day and left.

The old cannery manager's house was still in pretty good shape. The caretaker, a transplanted Dubliner by the name of Jack Cabina, lived there. He said the mice hadn't been a problem since he got the cat. There were a few managers' houses on the hill, and a suburb of sorts that was known as

New Town when it was built in the early 1960s. It was a collection of bungalows above a section of town known as Aroma Heights. There was the shell of a four-room schoolhouse, and below it the gymnasium, with its basketball court and what turned out to be the bowling alley.

But back at the mouth of the Namu River, just below the bridge, there is something else that remains, something that was there long before Robert Draney arrived with his big plans. You can see it at low tide. It's a row of rocks, the remnants of what was once a fish trap. All that can be said about its antiquity is that it was built sometime over the past 6,000 years. And there is another thing, although it's not here anymore. It's kept in a museum collection at Simon Fraser University. It isn't much to look at. It's just a tiny stone, smaller than an egg, but about the same shape, with a carved groove encircling it. It was unearthed from a trench, from just behind where the old bunkhouse used to be. It's most likely a sinker, from a fishing line. If it is, it is the oldest known piece of fishing gear in British Columbia. Probably some fisherman let it drop, unnoticed, out of his tackle-box, about 9,000 years ago. No matter what might be said of the cannery civilization that emerged and died over the space of a century on this coast, there is another, older civilization involved in this place. It is as old as any maritime culture on earth.

There is nothing much to account for it now, but at Namu, there is an unbroken chain of human experience spanning the last 11,000 years. It is the oldest known site of human occupation in British Columbia. It is probably the oldest continuously occupied site in Canada. The little egg-shaped stone might not seem like much, but it is a relic of something unique in human history. It flies in the face of all the conventional theories proposed by anthropologists about the history of human settlement on the planet. It defies closely-held notions about the way human societies are destined to behave.

As the historian Patricia Ann Berringer pointed out in her monumental 1982 study, *Northwest Coast Traditional Salmon Fisheries: Systems of*

Resource Utilization, "the northwest coast is an anomaly." It was enough of an anomaly, she concluded, that social scientists should rethink their classifications of non-industrial societies altogether. What was anomalous about northwest coast culture was that it was a civilization centred on the harvest of marine resources, and it was completely self-sustaining. Its maritime economies did not develop in association with, say, agricultural economies, as was the case with maritime civilizations from the Baltic Sea to the Peruvian coast. And the northwest coast also shared at least as much with highly stratified agricultural societies as with hunter-gatherer societies. The complex social structures associated with northwest coast societies were rigidly hierarchical, with densely populated villages and towns concentrated at rivermouths and river canyons.

Northwest coast culture is ancient. It was becoming widespread throughout North America's Pacific coast 6,000 years ago – about the same time that a tribe at a place called Thenai was emerging as the predominant tribe of Egypt, with its principal village at Memphis, and was starting to build pyramids. The northwest coast culture pattern had its origins in only a few villages, and one of those was Namu, which is one of the first fishing villages anywhere on earth. There was Namu, there were Mesolithic people settling down along the shores of the Baltic Sea, and the ancestors of the Egyptian Thenai who were setting out in dugouts from villages around the mouth of the Nile.

On British Columbia's coast, the northwest coast culture emerged towards the end of the chaos that characterized the early Holocene Epoch, when sea levels rose from the meltwater of shrinking glaciers, and the landscape was still rising and buckling and reshaping itself, relieved of the weight of Pleistocene ice sheets. There are memories of these early days that live on in the oral traditions of B.C.'s coastal peoples. Nuxalk stories, for instance, recount the Wanderings of Cormorant, who travels down to the open ocean and on to the land of the salmon. Cormorant turns north, and in his voyages he encounters landforms and forests and sea life

completely unlike anything one would encounter today. Haida Gwaii, for instance, was joined to the mainland by a broad, coastal plain, in a way that contemporary geologists understand the Queen Charlotte Islands were once connected to the mainland by something they prefer to call the Hecate Lowlands, a broad, windswept and undulating plain of scrubby trees.

In the memory of the people from Cape Caution to the Nass, there are stories of those early times, before order came to the world. There are stories of the Great Flood, and there are stories of the times that followed, when encampments became villages, and villages became towns, and the stories live on in chiefs' names, in dances, in crests and in placenames on the landscape. Beginning with those stories, what emerges are at least three major chapters in the human history of the coast. The first is a story about hunter-gatherers. The second is a story about a civilization founded upon fish and cedar. The third is the story of the cannery culture, its rise and fall, and the age we are now entering at the beginning of the 21st century.

In very early days, at Namu, there existed what might be reasonably described as a society of hunter-gatherers, although the people were remarkably dependent on marine life – sea mammals, shellfish, salmon and a variety of other finfish. But between 5,000 and 6,000 years ago, gradually-sloping beaches were beginning to form throughout the coast, creating clam beds, allowing for significant shellfish processing operations and a steady supply of food during the long winters. In 1967, George MacDonald, from the National Museum in Ottawa, was left scratching his head about how to make sense of it all after he calculated that Prince Rupert harbour, alone, contained about five million cubic feet of shell heaps.

It was also between 5,000 and 6,000 years ago that cedar became established as a dominant tree

One of the oldest known pieces of fishing equipment ever found in B.C. This stone may have been used as an anchor for a fishing line, and is estimated to be about 9,000 years old.
GARY FIEGEHEN

First Nations woman drying fish, Hagwilget, 1890s. Drying on wooden racks was a common form of preserving the catch.

BC ARCHIVES, # A-06051

From Cape Caution to the Tlingit fisheries, many "gear types" were used, but of these technologies, the most productive and efficient were traps, weirs and dams

species of the coastal forests, and it was the relationship between people and cedar that allowed the northwest coast culture pattern to fully flower. Cedar was the resource that allowed the construction of massive, permanent and semi-permanent houses, fish processing facilities and meeting halls. Ocean-going canoes were carved from cedar trees, and cedar provided the raw material for storage sheds, smokehouses, crates, boxes, tombs, hats, capes, ropes and tools.

One thing that was happening during this period that was at least as important as anything else involves the stone wall at the mouth of the Namu River, the one you can see at low tide. It is slightly curving, jutting out from the beach, and scattered around it are bits of broken glass and gnarled scraps of iron. It was about 6,000 years ago, 2,000 years before ancient Britons began building Stonehenge, that people all over this coast started building the kind of thing that remains in the remnant stone wall at the mouth of the Namu River. The classic northwest coast culture was being born.

"When people developed the fish trap, then, 'bang.' Once they developed that technology, well, things really took off after that," says Roy Carlson, an archaeologist who has been involved, in one way or another, in every archaeological excavation at Namu. There have been several. The first excavation was carried out by James Hester of the University of Colorado in 1969. Back then, Carlson was Hester's assistant. Hester's studies continued in 1970, and by 1977, archaeological field studies were being undertaken at Namu under Carlson's direction, and he headed further studies in 1978 and 1994. The work of Carlson and his colleagues confirmed the presence of people at Namu as early as 11,000 years ago, but it was the epoch beginning about 6,000 years ago that the fishery started going big-time. It was at about that time that a full-fledged, broadly based marine economy was flourishing at Namu, and it had started to flourish, from California to Alaska.

All this was not a simple matter of fishing in order to have something to eat. It was about the transformation of a perishable commodity into non-perishable wealth and status in an elaborate economic system based on balanced reciprocity. It was about maintaining ancient and complex relationships between people and animal spirits. It was about catching fish, preserving them, distributing them, accounting for their distribution in unwritten but precise ledgers, storing them, and organizing that kind of activity on such a massive scale as to build a civilization. It wasn't about anything very "hunter-gatherer" at all.

Patricia Ann Berringer's study is the only comprehensive analysis of the salmon-fishing technologies that were deployed throughout the northwest coast culture area, which ranges, very roughly, from the Eel River in California to Alaska's Yakutat Bay. Her research shows something of the effort involved in the construction and functioning of a civilization based on salmon. In the harvest sector alone, it involved hook-and-line trolling gear, beach seines, gillnets, trawls, gaffs, spears, harpoons, weirs, dip nets, reef nets, stone tidal traps, grid traps, cylindrical traps, tumbleback traps, box traps, basin traps, trough traps, log dams and stone dams.

From Cape Caution to the Tlingit fisheries, most of these "gear types" were used, but of these technologies, the most productive and efficient were traps, weirs and dams. They remained a dominant feature of the coast's fisheries until they were banned by the federal government, beginning with laws enacted in the 1880s. In 1968, J.A. Pomeroy, an archaeologist working with Carlson, identified 109 fishtrap sites of one sort or another in the Heiltsuk territory. Of the two dozen ancestral villages recorded in the oral traditions of the Heiltsuks' neighbours, the Nuxalks, all of them are associated with a fish trap.

Meanwhile, near the confluence of the Skeena and Bulkley Rivers, the Skeena narrows and roars through a gorge known as Hagwilget Canyon. It was the site of a significant and labour-intensive Gitxsan fishery, which also involved Wet'suwet'en harvesters who traditionally travelled to the canyon during the sockeye season. The technology consisted of an elaborate system of chutes suspended by ropes from log superstructures. As the violent current forced salmon against the canyon walls, the chutes formed a series of traps that were raised and lowered, each acting as a kind of mechanical flume that carried salmon into a series of wickerwork cages. The Hagwilget Canyon fishery was described briefly in 1905 by fisheries officer Hans Helgeson, whose reports were filed with the federal Department of Marine and Fisheries – the predecessor to Fisheries and Oceans Canada. Helgeson observed "numerous paths, stagings, ladders etc," at Hagwilget, where native people lined the canyon during the sockeye runs to harvest fish "with every possible contrivance," including traps suspended by ropes from stagings on the canyon walls.

Helgeson's reports provide a vivid account of some of the northwest coast's most elaborate large-scale trap fisheries – fisheries undertaken at fence-like weirs on the Kispiox, the Babine, the Blackwater, the Gitwangak and the Nass. Helgeson was primarily concerned with the complex of weirs

known as the "Babine Barricades," located on the Babine River, a tributary of the Skeena, and on tributaries to Babine Lake. The coastal cannery owners had persuaded federal fisheries managers that the native fisheries upriver were causing a labour shortage on the coast, and also that the barricades posed a conservation concern. Helgeson had been dispatched to the Babine in September of 1905 with instructions to enforce the law and dismantle as many weirs as he could.

Fish traps, Hagwilget, 1926. Native fish traps were highly effective tools. Archaeologists have uncovered evidence of ancient fish traps which may have been used 6,000 years ago.
BC ARCHIVES, # A-06010

Traditional Nisga'a salmon smokehouse. One smoke house could be filled from floor to ceiling with hundreds of fish.
GARY FIEGEHEN

"The barricades were constructed of an immense quantity of materials, on scientific principles," Helgeson reported.

On the Babine River: "There were posts driven into the bed of the river, which is 200 feet wide, and from two to four feet deep, and running swiftly at the intervals of 6 or 8 feet… Then sloping braces well bedded in the bottom and fastened to the top of posts, then strong stringers all the way on top and bottom, in front of posts, then panels beautifully made of slats woven together with bark set in front of all, these were set firmly into the bottom, and reaching 4 feet above the water… Altogether the barricades presented a most formidable and imposing appearance."

On his trip into the Upper Skeena watershed, Helgeson encountered a society that used dried sockeye as a form of currency, "a sort of legal tender," and its procurement was accomplished mainly at dams and weirs, which Helgeson's party encountered – and destroyed – on the Tatche River, the Tiltitcha River and the Fifteen-Mile River. On the Beaver River, Helgeson came upon what he called a barricade of a "peculiar" kind, which was a dam, through which a tunnel about two metres in width led to a "bin" that was retrieved by rope. Helgeson destroyed the Beaver River dam, too: "When we left, the river was full of material and debris for quite a distance."

The most elaborate of the weir fisheries Helgeson observed was the twinned barricade on the main stem of the Babine River, about 10 kilometres downstream from Babine Lake.

"The banks of the Babine River have a lovely appearance at this place and a most wonderful sight met our eyes when we beheld the immense array of dried salmon. On either side, there were no less than 16 houses 30 x 27 x 8 feet filled with salmon from the top down so low that one had to stoop to get into them and also an immense quantity of racks, filled up outside. If the latter had stood close together they would have covered acres and acres of ground, and though it was impossible to form an estimate, we judged it to be nearly three-quarters of a million fish at those two barricades, all killed before they had spawned, and though the whole tribe had been working together for six weeks and a half it was a wonder that so much salmon could be massed together in that time."

And these were just some of the salmon fisheries of the coast. For thousands of years, native societies engaged in harvests upon a staggering diversity of fish populations. In 1992, Roy Carlson conducted analyses of the faunal remains of 102 archaeological sites in B.C., most of them on the coast, spanning the past 11,000 years. Of the sites that yielded fish bones, salmon bones were found in three out of four sites; in half those sites, salmon bones comprised at least half the fish bones found. He concluded from this that, of the dizzying variety of fish available to people, salmon, not surprisingly, was the most important. At Namu, 88 per cent of the fish bones were salmon bones. They were tentatively identified as chum, coho and pink. Those are still the salmon species that spawn in the Namu River today.

But it wasn't all about salmon. Not by a long shot. Apart from salmon bones, what Carlson also found was that dogfish, of all things, was present at half the 102 sites surveyed. Most of those were spiny dogfish. While valued for its flesh and its oil, dogfish was also used for its skin, which was the "sandpaper" in the typical coastal woodworking toolkit. It's perfect for cedar. The oldest dogfish bones identified in Carlson's survey were 6,000 years old. Carlson found them himself, at Namu.

Herring bones showed up in 44 per cent of the fishbone sites – although herring bones don't last as long as whalebones, say, so those figures might not mean much. But herring bones at least 6,000 years old were found at Namu – the oldest herring bones discovered at any of the coast's archaeological sites. Next cames rockfish, which occured at 42 per cent of the sites. Rockfish bones found at Namu are the oldest rockfish bones found on the coast – 6,000 years old. Rockfish was followed by cod. Again, the oldest cod bones found on the coast were at Namu, at the 6,000-year level. Then came the flatfish, which include halibut, sole and flounder, and then came sculpins, ratfish (in surprising amounts), greenlings (including lingcod), ocean perch, skate, sturgeon, midshipman, minnows, suckers, oolichan, tuna, stickleback, prickleback, anchovy, wolf-fish, and shark.

And then there are marine resources that didn't show up among fishbones unearthed at archaeological sites. An example of that is herring roe, a prime delicacy harvested as "spawn-on-kelp" and "spawn-on-branches," which were fisheries that also involved the people of Namu. The thing about spawn-on-kelp and spawn-on-branches is that no bones are left because no fish are caught: Spawn is gathered from kelp, either after a "natural" spawn, or from kelp fronds suspended in the path of spawning herring. Spawn-on-branches is similar, except that hemlock branches, sometimes small hemlock trees, are sunk in the middle of a school of spawning herring, and the roe is later stripped from the branches.

The size of the human populations that these fisheries supported remains a subject of some conjecture, but recent research has allowed for a consensus among archaeologists that the northwest coast supported population densities higher than anywhere in North America north of the Valley of Mexico. British Columbia alone, according to University of British Columbia cultural geographer Cole Harris, was home to at least 200,000 people prior to the arrival of the first European explorers.

Recent studies of the marine-derived nitrogen content in human remains present a picture of cultures uniquely and overwhelmingly reliant upon fish. In a coast-wide study, archaeologist Brian Chisholm, working with archaeologist Erle Nelson and McMaster University geologist Henry Schwarcz, found that about 90 per cent of the protein in coastal peoples' diets came from the sea. The remains of 14 individuals from a single site were examined, and the protein in 13 of the 14 individuals showed that the marine-derived portion was a staggering 100 per cent. They were from Namu.

The volume of fish associated with the northwest coast's pre-industrial fisheries is a difficult thing to get a handle on. It is only recently that the amount of salmon associated with pre-industrial fisheries has been fully appreciated. The anthropologist Gordon Hewes, who first looked into the question while he was a doctoral student at the University of California at Berkeley in the 1940s, concluded in 1973 – based on the most conservative population estimates – that the tribal fisheries accounted for a staggering 127 million pounds of salmon, annually. To put that figure in context, it amounts to slightly more fish than the average annual commercial catch of sockeye on the B.C. coast during the 20th century. And throughout this century, much of that production – in many years, well more than half of it – was processed in little cannery towns all up and down B.C.'s coast, in towns like Namu.

Of all the perplexing questions that arise during a stroll through the ruins of towns like Namu, the easier questions to answer are the ones about how the first great coastal civilization collapsed, and how the cannery-town culture emerged from its ruins. The simplest answer is smallpox. Among the various European epidemic diseases that swept through the northwest – measles, chickenpox, influenza and others – by far the most devastating was smallpox. It is known that a wave of smallpox swept westward across the continent and arrived at the coast in 1792, at the

He concluded that, of the dizzying variety of fish available to people, salmon, not surprisingly, was the most important

mouth of the Columbia River, and then turned north. The oral traditions of Coast Salish native peoples contain vivid and heart-rending records of the event. It is also without question that smallpox decimated Tlingit villages, to the north of the Haida and Tsimshian territories, in the 1770s. It seems likely, however, that between Cape Caution and, say, the Haisla country around Kitamaat, smallpox did not arrive with any general ferocity until 1862.

Among the various European epidemic diseases that swept through the northwest – measles, chickenpox, influenza and others – by far the most devastating was smallpox

After the Fraser River gold rush of 1858 turned the sleepy precincts of Fort Camosun into the overnight boomtown of Victoria, the colonial capital was visited frequently by flotillas of canoes from throughout the coast. It was not uncommon, according to reports in the *British Colonist* newspaper of the time, for more than 2,000 "Hydahs," "Chimseans," "Bella Bellas" and "Stickeens" to be camped at the edge of town to trade, visit, and generally observe the strange spectacle that was unfolding there. There was no indication of the holocaust that was to follow from a report in the March 18, 1862 edition of the *Colonist* that a passenger aboard a steamer that had just arrived from San Francisco had brought a case of "varioloid" with him. The man had to postpone his plans to head for the Fraser River goldfields, but his condition was "not considered dangerous by the attending physician."

In the weeks that followed, the coast would be changed forever. By May of that year, the "varioloid," which was another term for smallpox, was reported to have killed three Fort Rupert people who had been visiting Victoria. Another 10 Tsimshian people who had succumbed to it were being treated at a tent clinic some missionaries had established. Seven Haida people were reported sick with it, and on May 12, the *Colonist* reported that two Haida people had died from smallpox. Within days, Victoria was a horrific scene, as native people fled the city in droves. White men evicted their own native "country wives," who lingered in the trees to be close to their children. Victoria's police commissioner ordered the Indian camps evacuated and burned. A police raid on a Haida encampment at Ogden Point found "a death-like stillness" and the smell of rotting flesh about the place. There was no one left to evict. There had been 100 people in the camp two weeks earlier; none were found alive.

In the following days, canoe flotillas were driven off the beaches around Victoria harbour. They headed out for Haro Strait, carrying hundreds of sick and terrified people, bound north, for home. Few made it. On June 14, the *Colonist* reported what the crew of the schooner *Nonpareil* had seen of the exodus: "As soon as pustules appear upon an occupant of one of the canoes, he is put ashore; a small piece of muslin, to serve as a tent, is raised over him, a small allowance of bread, fish and water doled out and he is left alone to die." A week later, the captain of the sloop *Northern Light* told the *Colonist* that the Kwageulths of Fort Rupert were "nearly exterminated," and 40 out of some 60 Haida people who had left Victoria in one flotilla in April had died en route.

Those that did make it home from Victoria brought the disease with them. In 1883, George Dawson, the geologist, surveyor and chronicler who spent most of his career with the Geological Survey of Canada, estimated that the Haida had been almost immediately reduced to about 2,000 people from a "pre-contact" population that exceeded 7,000, and their numbers were halved again, in the years that followed. It was the same, in village after village, all over the coast. Some villages were literally decimated – as much as 90 per cent of the population died. Other villages, perhaps most of the villages of the coast, were completely emptied.

It was into this post-holocaust landscape that the canneries came. First on the Sacramento River in California, then on the Columbia, then on the Fraser, and then, in the early 1870s, a certain William Woodcock settled in at a slough that branches off the north side of the mouth of the Skeena River, at the site of an old Tsimshian fishing village. Woodcock had no legal title to the land, but it didn't stop him from establishing a small trading post and an inn, and the place came to be called Woodcock's Landing. The property changed hands a few times over the years, and by 1876 it was held by the North Western Commercial Company, which proceeded immediately to build a cannery there, the first of several in a community that would come to be called Port Edward. The first cannery was called Inverness, and 40 oar-and-sail gillnet boats, crewed by white settlers and by local native people, mainly from the nearby Tsimshian community of Metlakatla, began hauling chinook and sockeye from the Tsimshians' prime fishing grounds in the vicinity. But the main workforce consisted of 225 shoreworkers, mainly Metlakatla women, who were employed processing the first fish ever to be put in cans north of Cape Caution. Inverness, which was to stay in business, in one form or another, for another 107 years, was shortly followed by the Aberdeen cannery, built by the Windsor Canning Company. By 1879, the Port Edward canneries were churning out 10,000 48-pound cases of canned salmon every year.

The coast's first canneries were generally owned by industrialists from New Westminster and Victoria. An exception to the rule was the Metlakatla cannery, built by the Metlakatla people, in their home community, in 1882. But then, everything about Metlakatla was exceptional. Led by the Methodist utopian William Duncan, Metlakatla had gas-lit streets, Victorian houses, a sawmill, a brickworks, a tannery, a brass band, its own uniformed police force, a jail, and a cathedral-sized church. Duncan had arrived in the apocalyptic hysteria that followed smallpox, and he promised order and a strange new religion that made sense of everything. In great measure, he lived up to his promises, but he eventually ran afoul of church officials, colonial authorities, and later the provincial government. Duncan and about 1,000 of his followers left for Alaska in 1887, a quarter-century after the peculiar socialist experiment began. They took almost everything with them, including the cannery.

By the late 1880s, salmon canning was taking the place of gold and furs as the new engine of British Columbia's coastal economy. Well before 1890, the Fraser River was already getting crowded, with more than a dozen canneries in operation, and the Scotsman Henry Bell-Irving led the first consolidation of the canneries in 1891. He acquired nine canneries, which he turned over to the "English syndicate" – the Anglo-British Columbia Packing Company (the "A.B.C." company) – establishing a pattern of expansion, corporate concentration, overfishing, contraction, re-expansion and more overfishing that remained a debilitating feature of the fishing industry throughout the 20th century.

One remedy to the Fraser's overcrowding was to simply move north, and the Inverness and Aberdeen canneries on the Skeena were soon joined by the Standard cannery, Balmoral, British American and others. By 1892, there were at least eight canneries in full swing around the mouth of the Skeena River, along with three others on the Nass River, one south of the Skeena at Lowe Inlet, and a handful at Rivers Inlet.

From these ramshackle and seat-of-the-pants beginnings, a new, polyglot culture was born. The managerial class was made up almost exclusively of white males, often recent arrivals from Great Britain. But the workforce was Tsimshian, Nisga'a, Haida, Heiltsuk, Nuxalk and Kwageulth. It was also Chinese, Japanese, English, French and Scandinavian. Native people became piece-workers and wage labourers almost overnight. The men fished, and the women worked at machines.

Like almost every cannery on the coast, Namu had its China House, a barn-like building to house Chinese workers who were indentured to a "China boss" that provided the cannery with labour. Almost all the Chinese cannery workers were young peasants from Canton who had fled that coastal city following the economic disruption that the Opium War caused throughout the Chinese economy. There are few harbours on B.C.'s coast where children have not scrambled through the ruins of old China Houses for the prize of an old, empty opium bottle. By the late 1800s, Canton had become a depressed place for the peasantry, and the city was clogged with unemployed artisans and craftsmen whose labour was made redundant by the oversupply of European trade goods. One of the few opportunities was emigration, and many of the first Chinese cannery workers were veterans of the Fraser River gold rush of 1858. Before the 20th century began, thousands of Cantonese peasants and artisans were labouring in B.C.'s canneries. On the Skeena, Henry Bell-Irving said, the typical cannery would have 15 white employees, 75 native men and women, and 75 Chinese men. The China boss, and the old labour-contract system, remained a feature of cannery life until half-way through the 20th century.

The story of the first Japanese cannery workers is similar to that of the Chinese in certain key respects: The Japanese were a racial minority, they were denied the vote until the 1940s, they were paid a fraction of a "white man's wage," and they did work that white people were loath to do. But the Japanese participation in the cannery culture was distinct. Japanese sailors and fishermen served the canneries as harvesters, rarely taking assembly-line work. They also laboured as boatbuilders. Many were as independent of the canneries as the law allowed, and their independence sometimes posed threats to white fishermen and native fishermen alike. Native communities felt particularly aggrieved by the arrival of hard-working Japanese fishermen who threatened to take over their exclusive preserve as chum salmon fishers on the north coast.

There are several archival sources that provide a picture of the kind of work involved in the coast's early canneries, and the organization of work, along with the cultural composition of the labour force, that remained largely unchanged through most of the 20th century. Typically, the fish were brought into the cannery either directly by the fishermen, or by a packer that collected the salmon from the fishing grounds. At the cannery, crews of native women went to work gutting the salmon and cutting off the heads and tails. From there, the fish went to a washing tank, where the fish were scrubbed and had their fins removed. Then they went for "sliming," which meant scrubbing the fish, and scraping out their insides. After another wash, the fish were then cut into can-sized pieces, first by Chinese crews, and later, after the invention of the mechanical gang knife known as the "Iron Chink," by machine. Native women did the work of stuffing the pieces into cans, and were paid by the number of trays of filled cans. The cans were then weighed, also by native women, and from there the cans went back to Chinese workers who were assigned the elaborate work of soldering, cooking, sealing and testing the cans. Generally, Chinese workers were also assigned the work of labelling the cans and packing them into cases. Where canneries built their own boxes, that was usually "Chinese work."

It was at a time when the whole coast was beginning to ring with these strange new sounds that Robert Draney arrived in the depopulated country of the Heiltsuk people, in 1893.

Robert Draney had emigrated from Ontario, and his first experience with salmon-canning was as a blacksmith at Inverness, at Woodcock's Landing. In 1882, in partnership with Victoria businessman Thomas Shotbolt, Draney supervised the construction of the first cannery on Rivers Inlet, in the territory of the Heiltsuk's neighbours, the Oweekeno people. Draney arrived on a winter day, in a blinding snowstorm, aboard the steamer *Barbara Boscourtz*. The cannery was to be built at a site they had named Shotbolt Bay, but when the snowstorm lifted the next day, Draney looked around and discovered that the steamer had left them about three miles from the intended site. Draney decided where they'd been left was good enough, and he and his construction crew went to work, and built the cannery there. Later that decade, the Rivers Inlet cannery was sold to the British Columbia Canning Company. Soon after, Draney arrived at Namu.

The reasons he chose Namu Harbour are obvious: sheltered from the open sea, affording protected anchorage for steamships, with enormous supplies of fresh water and solid, standing timber. Among the Heiltsuk people, there is still a dim memory of Draney's arrival at Namu. The place had been reduced to a small village, and there were still a few people living there when Draney put ashore. When archaeologists showed up in the 1970s, Heiltsuk elder Clarence Martin pointed out where some of the people's houses had been, and among Heiltsuk elders there persists a memory that Draney's presence was welcomed because of the promise of jobs a cannery would bring. Draney chose Namu with enthusiasm, and before long, Namu Harbour was ringing with the strange sounds of the industrial revolution.

Henry Doyle, the founding manager of the B.C. Packers Association, said Draney's choice of Namu was made "judiciously," because "it lay about half-way between Queen Charlotte and Milbanke sounds, [and] all the territorial area between these waterways, with its immense fishery wealth, was tributary to the seat of his operations." Draney settled in with his wife and young family, and raised six sons and a daughter at Namu. Considering his growing family, Draney built a second cannery, at Kimsquit, in 1902. In its early years, Namu was one of the best equipped and most self-sufficient cannery towns on the coast. It was the first cannery to install its own can-making machinery; cans made at Namu were also used at Kimsquit. Doyle, who was notoriously cantankerous, had this to say of Draney: "Robert and Mrs. Draney were noted all along the northern British

Fishermen mending dogfish nets, Queen Charlotte City, 1947. The abundance of fish along the north west coast attracted many entrepreneurs. Canneries started appearing along the coast in the late 1800s.
BC ARCHIVES, # I-22212

There was salmon to be had – along with halibut, clams, herring and other species

Columbia coast for their genial and open-hearted hospitality, and Namu in their time was always the mecca toward which all transient travellers turned."

Doyle, a voracious consolidator who was the prime mover in the establishment of the B.C. Packers Association in 1902, went on a disastrous buying spree during the First World War. Among the properties Doyle acquired were Draney's canneries at Namu and at Kimsquit. That was in 1912; the following year, Doyle found himself in deep financial trouble, and by 1915, R.V. Winch and Company had acquired a 52 per cent interest in Draney's former operations, with Doyle holding the remainder.

In the early years of this century, the frenzy of cannery-building between Cape Caution and the Nass River followed a pattern that had been established by the Fraser River gold rush. There was salmon to be had – along with halibut, clams, herring and other species – and a ready market among the booming mill towns the industrial revolution was throwing up all over the northern hemisphere.

Fish were a resource to be mined. In 1913 – the same year that railroad crews blasted the side of a mountain into Hell's Gate, in the Fraser canyon – the commercial catch of Fraser River sockeye reached 30 million fish. The Fraser all but collapsed. The First World War produced a massive demand for canned salmon, and markets for canned chum and canned pink salmon were rapidly expanding. B.C.'s central coast was rich with these species, and the rush north, with canneries popping up in cove after cove, was in full swing. By 1915, the Native Fishing Association could claim 500 members, mainly gillnet fishermen, from 21 coastal communities, most of them on the central coast.

The cannery boom did not end when the war ended.

By 1921, there were more than 6,000 gillnet and troll fishermen on B.C.'s coast. About 1,200 of these fishermen were native people, and almost all of them were fishing with boats and licences owned by the canneries operating north of Cape Caution. There were more than 2,200 white fishermen in the fleet, and about half of them fished for the canneries north of Cape Caution. The final 2,600 vessels were operated by Japanese fishermen, and more than 1,000 of these were fishing for the northern canneries. The World War I veterans, who had returned to the coast in the thousands only to find joblessness, were turning in increasing numbers to the fishery. These were white males, and they had little time for the canners' preferences for cheap, vulnerable non-white labour. Through "yellow-peril" scares and racist agitation – a habit that many white fishermen would find hard to shake through most of the 20th century – the federal government was persuaded to set about the work of limiting the Japanese presence in the fleet. The northern canneries, particularly, exploited these policies to their advantage: each cannery was granted an "allotment" of Japanese fishermen, who were prized not just because of their skills, but because they could be paid half the piece rates for fish that white fishermen were paid.

Salmon cans ready for lacquer, McTavish Cannery, Rivers Inlet, 1920. Canneries employed First Nations people and immigrants from England, France, China and Japan.
BC ARCHIVES, # H-06490

These were busy years at Namu. After Doyle's buying-spree troubles, he went into partnership with Winch, and together, by 1918, their jointly-owned Northern British Columbia Fisheries Ltd. consisted of Namu and Kimsquit, the canneries at Kincolith and Kumeon on the Nass, the Commercial cannery on the Skeena River, and canneries at Tallheo, near Bella Coola, and at Port Edward. Doyle's fortunes did not improve with Northern B.C. Fisheries, however, partly because of his own preoccupation with expansion and consolidation, and partly because of the intrigues among the fraternity of cannery owners, within which there was rarely much in the way of honour. One of Doyle's occasional comrades-in-arms during various internecine wars of attrition and merger was Aemilius Jarvis, who spent much of the 1920s in prison, in Ontario, for stock fraud. Jarvis was also the founding president of B.C. Packers Ltd., the successor to Doyle's B.C. Packers' Association.

It was at Namu that Doyle's grand schemes went awry. In 1923, Namu's entire production spoiled, and the setback brought the house down around both Doyle and Winch. In 1924, Namu, which Doyle had described as "the company's best asset," was sold, on instructions from the Royal Bank, which also ordered the rest of Northern B.C. Fisheries' properties sold or leased. The Gosse-Millerd Company bought the Namu operations for $180,000 – an amount it raised from an insurance claim after its cannery at East Bella Bella burned to the waterline. To say the least, the Namu deal was a bargain: The General Appraisal Company of Seattle had reckoned Namu's assets at $332,000.

The loss of Namu infuriated Doyle. He had described Namu as "the best plant in British Columbia," because of its assets and its fortuitous location. "The cannery is one of the largest and best-equipped in the province," Doyle wrote, "and under proper management can pack 75,000 to 100,000 cases annually. In addition, there is a sawmill and a box factory at which all the company's requirements in salmon boxes, etc., are manufactured." A "case" of salmon, despite variations in can sizes, was always 48

pounds of fish. Doyle's estimate of Namu's peak 1920s' capacity, then, was roughly 4,800,000 pounds of salmon, or slightly less than the weight of a million sockeye, annually. The loss of Namu must have upset Doyle enormously.

Not only were the 1920s boom years for cannery owners all over the coast, but a new invention, a mechanical gang knife known as the "Iron Chink" – so named because it did the work of a half-dozen Chinese labourers – reduced the labour cost per case by at least $2. The racial mix that characterized the cannery workforce was related directly to the canneries' labour costs, as illustrated by a labour-cost summary assembled by J.H. Todd and Sons for its Klemtu cannery, just a few sea miles from Namu. More than 30 white men were employed at Klemtu, including engineers, machinists, carpenters, electricians and other tradesmen. Salaries ranged from $170 per month for the oil plant operator to $295 a month for the netloft boss. There were 50 women employed at Klemtu, and 41 of them were native. They included slimers, washers, filling machine feeders and can-loft hands, and although it's difficult to compare salaries to the piece-rate pay that characterized "klootchman" (native women) labour, women were generally paid less than half what white males were paid. Klemtu also employed six native men in the cannery netloft, at rates ranging from $1.12 to $1.75 an hour, along with 54 Chinese men, who worked as butchers, "Iron Chink" feeders, box makers, and general labourers. The highest paid Chinese employee at Klemtu was the messhouse cook, who earned $185 a month, slightly more than the lowest-paid white male worker.

By half way through the 1920s, there were more than 70 canneries in operation on B.C.'s coast. But when the boom started showing signs of becoming a rapid and frightening bust, cannery owners started to talk to one another about how to

The racial mix that characterized the cannery workforce was related directly to the canneries' labour costs

put all the silly business of competition behind them to protect their investments. In 1928, out of the shell of Doyle's old B.C. Packers Association, Wallace Fisheries, and the former Gosse-Millerd assets – which included Namu – a new company was born. It was called B.C. Packers Ltd., and it was incorporated in New Jersey, which had some of the weakest anti-trust laws on the continent. Its founding president was Aemilius Jarvis, the convicted Ontario stock fraud. A single company now owned 44 coastal canneries.

One of the new company's first decisions was to consolidate its operations, and immediately, eight canneries were closed for good. Meanwhile, the Canadian Fishing Company (Canfisco), which had focused on halibut until 1918, had become a major player in the fish-canning business. By the 1920s, Canfisco was undertaking the same buy-consolidate-close strategy. Canfisco had shut down 10 of its 15 plants within five years of the 1928 shakedown. The dominance of B.C. Packers and the Canadian Fishing Company, which was firmly

established by the time the stock markets crashed in 1929, remained the central corporate feature of the fishing industry on B.C.'s coast for the rest of the 20th century.

The next big shakedown occurred in the late 1960s. By then, one of the last of the original firms still outside the ambit of B.C. Packers and Canfisco was the A.B.C. company, a remnant of Henry Bell-Irving's "English syndicate," which had pioneered the practice of expansion and consolidation with its acquisition of nine canneries in 1891. In 1969, B.C. Packers and Canfisco teamed up and bought out what was left of A.B.C., and immediately, the Klemtu cannery was shut down, along with Butedale. Those two cannery closures were followed by the dismantling of plants at Rivers Inlet, Sooke, and on the Skeena (see map 2.2). By 1971, Namu was no longer in the business of canning fish, and its final years as a fish-buying station, a supply point and a cold-storage facility had begun. Canfisco shut down the North Pacific cannery in Prince Rupert, and among the assets the company shed were 150 small gillnet boats that had been operated by native people from communities like Bella Bella and Klemtu.

In the same way that the 1923 spoilage of Namu's salmon pack precipitated a nasty shakeup for Doyle's fortunes, a 1962 fire, which destroyed the old cannery at Namu, also ended up redefining B.C. Packers' grip on the coast's fish-processing capacity. After the fire, B.C. Packers' insurers ordered that the entire cannery be rebuilt – an investment that drained B.C. Packers of its capital reserves and significantly weakened the company. Before the year was out, Namu – along with all the rest of B.C. Packers' properties – ended up in the hands of the Weston Foods conglomerate, one of the world's largest merchandising and retailing firms. B.C. Packers had become just another subsidiary, stocking the shelves of Weston's retail empire with cans of salmon, under a variety of "brand names," including the famous Clover Leaf trademark. From then on, B.C. Packers was a mere cog in the Weston machine.

In 1980, B.C. Packers started acquiring major pieces of Canfisco, including the Oceanside cannery in Prince Rupert. These purchases were followed by further closures and consolidations. In 1981, B.C. Packers pulled out of Port Edward, the same year it bought Petersburgh Processors in Alaska, establishing a foothold in the Alaskan fisheries that it later expanded.

By the late 1980s, Namu was starting to look more like a gas station than the boisterous fishing industry town it had been for almost a century, and there is something undeniably pathetic about how such a remarkable experience, with all its great promise, based on such great natural wealth, slowly crumbled into nothing. By the late 1990s, in the collapsing buildings down at the fuel supply dock, Namu's last days were recorded in copies of fuel-dock receipts, stacked in heaps, forgotten in a mouldy heap, in a closet.

On May 3, 1988, the famous Indian village mission boat, the *Thomas Crosby V*, put in and took on 450.1 gallons of diesel, paying $765.17. On May 10, the *Cloudburst* put in and bought $172.55 in diesel fuel and paid $7.13 for four-and-a-half gallons of stove oil. On May 30, the *Niska* stopped by and picked up $112 worth of gasoline, $3.21 in stove oil, a grease tube for $2.50 and $3.50 for a gallon of kerosene. Paid cash.

And then it was over.

It ended because of consolidation, the advent of centralized canning and cold-storage capacity, rapid technological advances in the harvesting and transportation of raw fish, a rapid shift away from the production of canned salmon and increased attention paid to the burgeoning world-wide market in fresh and frozen fish products. All these developments are routinely cited as the cause of the decline of the cannery culture. But these are not the underlying reasons why B.C.'s coastal communities were largely abandoned by the industry that sustained them for more than a century. The reasons for that lie in the corporate model that governments allowed to organize the extraction and processing of the coast's natural resources.

Apart from their access to large pools of capital, the advantage that corporations like B.C. Packers and Canfisco held over small companies, fish-dependent coastal communities and "cottage industry" processors, lay in a federal licensing system which allowed processors to own fishing licences. By the late 1990s, there were only about 2,600 vessels licenced to harvest salmon on the entire coast. Of those boats, slightly more than 400 were seine vessels, and they accounted for about half of all the salmon caught on Canada's west coast. The coast's seine vessels were becoming almost exclusively deep-draught, high-tech aluminum outfits, and about one-third of the boats were owned directly by B.C. Packers and Canfisco. By various contractual and service agreements with other boats, the two companies had come to control about 60 per cent of the harvesting and processing of salmon on the coast,

> **The advantage that corporations held...lay in a federal licensing system which allowed processors to own fishing licences**

Throughout this history of mergers, acquisitions, consolidations and plant closures, fishermen, along with their home communities, were left with the scraps

creating a situation in which two men, Galen Weston (B.C. Packers) and Jimmy Pattison (Canfisco), represented more than half of what was still quaintly described as B.C.'s commercial salmon fishing industry.

By the 1990s, B.C. Packers and Canfisco had given up any pretence of competition. The two firms had combined most of their buying and processing operations under the "Allied Processors" flag. Between them, Weston, Pattison and a few smaller companies exerted tremendous influence over the price paid to fishermen for salmon, in several ways. The most obvious way was by owning or controlling more than half the fleet to begin with. Another advantage lay in the fact that salmon fishing was usually a matter of having no fish, and then having so many fish all at once that the only way to move them was to a single, major buyer (and there are fewer and fewer buyers capable of handling significant volumes of salmon). Weston, through Nelbro Packing Company Ltd., also became one of the major players in the Alaskan salmon fishery, which almost always set the world price for sockeye and pink salmon.

Weston also invested heavily in salmon farming – the single greatest economic millstone around the necks of the small-boat salmon fishermen on the B.C. coast. The aquaculture gold rush has caused staggering declines in the market value of wild salmon, making it near to impossible for old-fashioned, small-boat fishermen to stay in the fishery. Weston's aquaculture holdings came to include operations in Chile, and mortgages and partial ownerships involving fish-farm companies such as Barkley Seafarms and Sea Spring Salmon Farm Ltd. By 1996, B.C. Packers alone held 18 separate netcage fish-farm leases on the B.C. coast, making the company the second largest netcage leaseholder in B.C. Closing the loop, Weston and Pattison, between them, practically owned the retail market.

They owned Save-On-Foods, the Great Canadian Superstore, SuperValu, Loblaws, and a variety of smaller retail chains.

And then, on March 4, 1999, the inevitable occurred. The Weston Corporation had decided to get out of wild salmon altogether, and in a terse announcement, Canfisco revealed that it had acquired B.C. Packers, along with Nelbro Packing's operations in Alaska and Washington state, all of B.C. Packers' interests in fishing vessels, Allied Pacific Processors and Alaska General Processors. Canfisco took all of it, including B.C. Packers' interests in the herring fleet. It was an event as historically significant, for the B.C. coast, as the merger of the Northwest Company with the Hudson's Bay Company in the early 1800s. But it barely warranted notice in the Vancouver news media. After all, throughout the 1990s, wild salmon landings had not once accounted for one half of one per cent of the gross provincial product.

Throughout this history of mergers, acquisitions, consolidations and plant closures, fishermen, along with their home communities, were left with the scraps. Between 1985 and 1993, the average earnings for a commercial fisherman in British Columbia went from slightly more than $10,000 in fishery-related income to slightly less than $10,000 in fishery-related income. Most fishermen made most of their earnings from a combination of employment insurance checks and odd jobs they could scratch together between seasons. The toll in human tragedy wrought by the consolidations and closures of canneries and fishplants up and down B.C.'s coast is difficult to describe in words. In 1954, almost half of all B.C.'s Indians identified the commercial fishing industry as their primary source of income. Another 20 per cent of native people responding to an occupational census conducted that year reported that the commercial fishing industry was their main source of supplementary income. Within 20 years, half those jobs were gone. Canneries and fishplants kept closing, sometimes one by one, sometimes by the handful, and the consequences were staggering. The Heiltsuk elder Mary

Hopkins put it this way, in an interview with Ulli Steltzer and Catherine Kerr, in 1982: "When the canneries were closed, there is no more jobs for us. All the women have time. We were really sad when we heard it; some of them cried. Now we only get welfare. I get old-age pension."

At the end of the 20th century, there was precious little left of Namu.

At one end of Namu Harbour, what remained of Tunerville was being taken back by the forest. Tunerville lay just beyond the harbour's old boat-yard and marine railways, which were collapsing into the harbour with every rising tide, and eight little houses were still standing there. It was obvious they were pretty once, whitewashed, with decorative trim and green shutters, but the paint had come to hang from living room ceilings like delicate white stalactites. Tunerville was still connected by several kilometres of rotting cedar boardwalk and bramble-covered footbridge to the rest of Namu Harbour, except where the boardwalk collapsed and became part of the forest. This is what happened on the far side of Namu River, just beyond the Indian houses, which were barely standing and contained nothing more than rusty spring bunkbeds, crumbling oil stoves and the occasional old refrigerator. Right about the place where a sign announced Bridge Over Cooch's Gulch, the boardwalk simply disappeared into the salal and willow, so to go on to the other end of the harbour you had to bushwack down to the beach and tread carefully across the rubble and detritus of old netguards, pottery shards, bits of sky-blue Chinese porcelain, fragments of seine net and trolling line, chain, and batteries.

All that was left down there was the rickety old marine-supply warehouse and fuel dock. This is the side of the harbour where the Japanese boats had their moorings. The Chinese houses were there once, too. There was no sign of either. The Japanese houses burned down in the early 1990s, along with the old netloft and the main bunkhouse. The old freezer plant still stood, and so did the cold storage buildings and the warehouse, despite cracks in the cement cinderblock. Inside was a jumble of herring freezer boxes, pallets, fish carts, broken-down forklifts and barrels of hydraulic oil.

Declining fish prices, fleet reduction schemes, mechanization, plant closures and the centralization of the industry in the Lower Mainland all took their toll on the coast. From the 1970s on, the fishing industry declined in its relative importance to other sources of income for the people of communities like Prince Rupert, Masset and Port Edward. But

Crumbling buildings and boardwalks are all that is left of the once prosperous cannery in Namu.
DAVE NUNUK

Fishing nets out to dry in Bella Coola. By 1993, 142 of the 9,663 separate stocks of salmon were extinct, and 932 others were considered to be at risk. GARY FIEGEHEN

through the 1980s, and well into the 1990s, the landed value of fish harvested between the northern tip of Vancouver Island and the Nass River remained quite stable, only occasionally falling below $200-million a year, usually close to half the landed value of all fish harvested on B.C.'s coast. Although its relative importance was declining, salmon remained the staple of the north coast's fisheries through the 1990s. Salmon was followed by herring, halibut, a variety of trawl-caught species, black cod, and other, minor fisheries, such as crab, prawn, geoduck, sea cucumber and sea urchin.

In the century that the Industrial Age held sway north of Cape Caution, tremendous damage was inflicted upon many fish populations, and in some cases, the damage was so severe that biologists can't say with any certainty whether recoveries are possible. Damage that extreme had been confined almost exclusively to distinct genetic populations within species, not to entire species. But biologists are often resigned to scratching their heads about the simplest of questions, as Tim Slaney, of Aquatic Resources Ltd., found in 1996. Working with a team of biologists from the American Fisheries

Society's North Pacific chapter, Slaney conducted a survey that identified 9,663 separate stocks of salmon and anadromous trout in British Columbia and the Yukon, but reliable data was available for only 57 per cent of those stocks. Still, 142 stocks were found to have become extinct. Another 624 stocks were classified as being at "high risk" of extinction, 78 were found to be of "moderate risk" and 230 were of "special concern." The data Slaney compiled was up-to-date as of 1993. A simple question might be, "How have those at-risk stocks fared since 1993?" Slaney's answer in 1998 was, "Nobody knows." Most of those stocks are small stocks, and the Department of Fisheries and Oceans doesn't monitor them regularly.

Most of the troubled salmon populations identified in Slaney's survey were from river systems south of Cape Caution, but casual conversations with any long-time north coast fisherman about stock declines will invariably lead to first-hand accounts of salmon runs that have been fished out, or are so badly damaged that DFO doesn't even know whether they are there anymore. These are "anecdotal" reports, however, and like years of complaints from Newfoundland's small-boat inshore fishermen about how the cod seemed to be disappearing, anecdotal reports from B.C. salmon fishermen have tended to be ignored in DFO's stock-assessment process. One decline that was impossible to ignore, however, was Skeena River coho. And Skeena coho – while suffering poor ocean survival rates, like most of the coast's coho – was particularly hard hit because of "mixed stock" fishing.

When weirs and traps gave way to rivermouth gillnets and saltwater seining and trolling, the "centre of fishing effort," as biologists call it, moved downstream into "mixed-stock" fishing areas. What this means is that most of the fish harvested from any given salmon run is harvested in waters where fish from several runs mingle and migrate together before branching off into their own separate runs. By applying the burden of fishing pressure in those downstream mixed-stock areas, fisheries conducted upon relatively abundant salmon runs, like Skeena sockeye, ended up taking unsustainably high numbers of small and vulnerable salmon runs, like Skeena River coho.

Beginning in the 1980s, native communities, conservationists and anglers routinely protested and complained about steelhead and coho declines in the Skeena. Then, in the 1990s, federal fisheries managers began a series of attempts to open a corridor for Skeena coho through the net gauntlet of the sockeye fisheries in the Lower Skeena and off the Skeena mouth. These attempts were largely confined to live-release rules for net-caught coho and steelhead, gear-modification experiments, and area closures. The conservation measures were timid, but they provoked a rowdy chorus of complaints from commercial fishermen.

By the late 1990s, while the arguments continued, coho were dropping off the edges of DFO's population-status charts. In 1997, after centuries of returns in the thousands, only 12 coho were caught in the Upper Bulkley River. On the Babine River, a Skeena tributary, coho spawners had been declining steadily since the 1960s. By 1998, a DFO discussion paper described Babine coho as "probably two orders of magnitude (1/100th) of the pre-1970 population size." DFO's northern stock status summary identified a "severe conservation problem" for Upper Bulkley, Babine, Sustut-Bear and other Skeena coho populations, and liberally used the word "crisis" to describe the situation. The summary identified poor marine survival rates, Alaskan interception and "chronic overfishing" in Canadian waters as the causes. DFO biologist Blair Holtby, in his own assessment of the prospects for Upper Skeena coho, warned that any catch of any Upper Skeena coho, by anyone, represented "a high risk to the viability of coho populations in that area." In the typically restrained language of DFO's salmon biologists, Holtby's report included these words: "We recommend a more conservative approach to the harvest of these coho stocks."

North of Cape Caution, there have been massive extirpations of various salmon species (see map 2.1). At the beginning of the 21st century, the coast's small-stock salmon runs were still reeling from decades of "creek-robbing" seine fisheries – a fish-mining practice that was not uncommon during the 1960s and 1970s, when a seiner from some distant port would put in at the mouth of a remote creek and haul sets all day until the hold was filled and there were no more fish. But there were other forces at work as well.

It is without question that the chronic overfishing and intermittent "fish wars" associated with the failed Canada-U.S. salmon treaty took their toll upon coho, chinook and steelhead salmon north of Cape Caution, particularly upon salmon bound for the Skeena River. So it was with great relief that many fishermen and conservationists greeted the announcement in 1999 that a new salmon treaty had been concluded between Canada and the United States. But, as details of the treaty become public, much of that relief turned to further anxiety. Tangible benefits of the treaty included a reduction in the American harvest of Skeena-bound sockeye, cooperative scientific and fisheries-management regimes, special funds for habitat restoration and protection, and provisions for dispute resolution. But the treaty also entrenched the previous agreement's mixed-stock fisheries, and Canada agreed to management measures designed to protect only "aggregate abundances" of chinook and coho salmon bound for north coast rivers. Because so few Canadian chinook and coho populations were included as index populations by which abundance could be monitored and fishing restraints imposed, many conservationists alleged that Canada had given up any attempts to conserve the spatial and genetic diversity of coho and chinook salmon.

But creek-robbing and "fish wars" do not explain the widespread and precipitous declines in salmon abundance throughout B.C.'s central coast – that labyrinth of channels and passages between Cape Caution and Kitimat.

Creek-robbing and "fish wars" do not explain the widespread and precipitous declines in salmon abundance throughout B.C.'s central coast

Unlike trends in Nass and Skeena sockeye abundance – which, except for a perplexing record-low return of Skeena sockeye in 1998, were generally stable through the 1990s – sockeye runs in the central coast all but vanished during the last decade of the 20th century. And most other salmon species in the area exhibited dramatic declines as well. Habitat destruction was certainly not a primary culprit – much of the region remains unlogged – and most salmon biologists agreed that a range of factors, including changes in the ocean environment, were responsible for the declines. Net fisheries that once lasted several months of the year in Whale Channel had been cut to a few days fishing in the 1990s, exclusively for pink and chum salmon. By the end of the 20th century, there were only a few salmon fisheries left anywhere in the central coast area – a few days a year in Fitz Hugh Channel, Spiller Channel, Roscoe Inlet, and Finlayson Channel, and perhaps a few days at Mathieson Channel, Mussell Inlet, McLoughlin Bay, and at the mouth of the Bella Coola. The tragic fact is that by the close of the 20th century, there were simply few salmon left to catch.

In the central coast area, there are an estimated 1,700 spawning populations of salmon. Fisheries and Oceans knew very little about them to begin with, but what they did know, by the late 1990s, was that broad-scale, dramatic declines were underway throughout the area, among all salmon species.

Rivers Inlet sockeye once attracted the third-largest sockeye fishery on the B.C. coast, in some years matching the Fraser and Skeena fisheries. In the 1950s, as many as three million sockeye returned to Rivers Inlet, headed for the spawning grounds in Oweekeno Lake. In 1999, a mere 3,500 spawners returned to spawn in Oweekeno Lake, and sockeye runs bound for Long Lake, at the head of nearby Smith Inlet, declined just as rapidly and

By 1999, the situation had become so stark that grizzly bears were starving through-out the region, and 14 grizzly bears had to be shot in and around Oweekeno village

dramatically. By 1999, the situation had become so stark that grizzly bears were starving throughout the region, and 14 grizzly bears had to be shot in and around Oweekeno village. On the Quaal River, pink salmon runs fell from 250,000 in the late 1980s to 80,000 in the late 1990s. On the Skowquiltz River, chum salmon declined from an average of 18,000 in the 1950s to fewer than 1,000 by the 1980s. Chum salmon bound for the Namu River fell from a 1950s' average of 17,000 to fewer than 4,000 in the 1990s. On the Aaltanhash River, coho runs fell from an average stock size exceeding 800 in the 1980s to fewer than 100 in the 1990s. And on it went.

While there hasn't yet been a complete extirpation of any fish species north of Cape Caution, one species that came close was abalone. Once a precious delicacy among native communities, and treasured as well by local settlers, the coast's abalone stocks suffered a classic gold-rush assault through the 1980s. More than 70,000 pounds of abalone were taken out of northern waters every year. Abalone was fetching up to $13.60 per pound to the fisherman by the time the entire coast was closed to abalone fishing in 1990. A decade later, there was still no sign of recovery.

There was a time, as recently as the late 1960s, when B.C.'s herring population had been pushed close to the same precarious place as abalone. Shortly after World War II, the coast's expanding seine fleet undertook a herring "reduction" fishery to produce fish oil and fishmeal – mainly for fertilizer and animal feed. By the 1960s, the reduction fishery accounted for catches as great as 250,000 tons a year – an amount roughly double the weight of British Columbia's human population at the time. The fishery crashed in 1967. Only then did DFO close the coast to herring fishing.

Five years after the closure, herring populations were already making localized recoveries, and a limited, small-scale fishery, exclusively for herring roe, was authorized to meet the demands of the Japanese delicacy market. In most places on the northwest coast, herring have returned, and in places, herring have returned in some abundance. Throughout the 1990s, fisheries managers routinely failed to keep the coast-wide herring roe fishery within its annual catch limits, however, and overharvesting of local herring populations remains a controversy on the coast. On the Queen Charlotte Islands, overfishing, local closures and bitter disputes between Haida fishermen and the Department of Fisheries and Oceans were commonplace through the 1990s. In 1998, a dispute erupted after DFO officials authorized a herring roe fishery in Haida waters that Haida fishermen said would seriously harm local stocks. There were several tense days of negotiations as Haida fishermen warned they would blockade boats, and the RCMP was called in to keep the peace. Ron Brown, then-president of the Council of the Haida Nation, explained: "They have never really given us a real say in anything in the management of any resource. No matter what our concerns are, they would still just send us a thing saying, 'There is going to be a commercial opening' at some time of year, and 'This much is going to be taken,' and that's it."

But at least the herring are still there. Between 1982 and 1993, herring roe harvested by gillnetters and seiners on the northwest coast produced an annual average landed value of $38-million, roughly half the coast-wide landings. More than half the northwest coast catch usually comes from the Heiltsuk and Kitasoo fishing grounds in the southern portion of DFO's North Coast District, and from the Tsimshian's fishing grounds, within a few sea miles of Prince Rupert.

By the 1990s, despite all the romanticism about a "threatened way of life" that usually accompanies public discourse about the difficulties of the west coast's commercial fishing industry, there really wasn't much of a way of life left.

From the early 1900s onward, federal fisheries policy was formed and shaped by practically every wish list the coast's major processors have ever assembled. Starting in the 1960s, the federal government began to defend its assistance to the near-monopoly of the coast's fishing companies by arguing that the myriad problems besetting the industry could be boiled down to "too many boats chasing too few fish." Under Fisheries Minister Jack Davis, the first major fleet-reduction program was initiated, and the abandonment of coastal communities, both native and non-native, was accelerated – not by accident, but as a matter of policy. Before the "Davis Plan," there were more than 6,000 salmon-licenced boats on the coast. After the Davis Plan, there were about 4,500. But fleet reduction did nothing to ease fishing pressure on vulnerable stocks, and accomplished even less in addressing the chronic problem of fleet overcapacity: the Davis Plan allowed the number of seine boats to double, and most of the boats driven out of the fleet were low-impact small boats, trollers and gillnetters. Native communities were hit the hardest.

Through the 1970s and 1980s, the industry became increasingly an urban-based affair, operating seasonally out of Vancouver and Prince Rupert, in the form of company-owned boats that fished a few weeks, sometimes a few days, every year, to supply the raw resources for the processing, wholesaling and retailing operations of the same companies. "Fleet reduction" has served the

Mending nets in Kincolith. Between the 1960s and the 1990s, the government of Canada reduced the number of salmon-licensed boats from 6,000 to 2,600. First Nations along the coast suffered the most from this dramatic reduction. GARY FIEGEHEN

As bizarre as it seems, in the 21st century, non-native communities along B.C.'s coast have no rights of access to the marine resources surrounding them

same cause that the federal government served in the early 1900s, when compliant politicians minimized the canners' labour costs by legislating exemptions from labour laws, providing a supply of disenfranchised immigrant workers, and surrendering control over boat licensing. Access to the fisheries resource remains a matter of money, not local tradition or long-standing customary laws. By limiting entry to the salmon fisheries, and then further limiting entry through fleet-reduction, the fishery became, increasingly, the private preserve of companies that could afford to accumulate boats and licences.

In the late 1990s, another fleet-reduction scheme was implemented, this time called the "Mifflin Plan," after Fisheries Minister Fred Mifflin. The Mifflin Plan reduced the fleet from about 4,500 to 3,000 vessels, then to fewer than 2,600 vessels, more than half of which were owned by Vancouver firms and residents of the Lower

Mainland. As it was with the Davis Plan, most of the boats that were shed from the fleet during the 1990s were older, smaller, low-impact boats. And as it was under Davis, native communities were hardest hit. A dozen licenced fishing vessels were lost in the villages of Bella Bella and Klemtu. Of the 50 fishboats that were lost to the Skeena, at least 16 were boats disappeared from the Tsimshian-area villages. On the Queen Charlotte Islands, a dozen licenced boats disappeared. At Kitkatla, about 50 sea miles south of Prince Rupert, there were more than 40 commercial salmon vessels in the 1950s. After the Davis plan, the Mifflin Plan and their successor programs, Kitkatla was left with a single seine boat owned by the Kitkatla Indian band and a half-dozen gillnet boats owned by band members.

Other elements of the Mifflin Plan – licence "stacking" and area-licensing requirements – ensure that the fleet will continue to grow smaller and more urban-based, and even more of a rich man's game. While some form of area licensing was long overdue, the combined effects of "stacking" and area licensing have produced results that can only

Wooden boats were replaced by modern aluminum boats, which could catch more fish with a smaller crew. As a result, the number of people employed in the fishery was greatly reduced. Fisherman's wharf at Prince Rupert Harbour, 1947.
BC ARCHIVES, # I-22250

benefit companies and individuals with access to big money, and will continue to drive out fishermen who never caught many fish in the first place.

Area-licensing divided the coast into three areas for gillnetters, three areas for trollers, and two areas for the big-boat seine fleet. Each boat can only fish one area, unless a licence is bought from another boat – which must then leave the fleet – and is "stacked" on the buyer's licenced vessel. In this way, gillnetters and trollers who were accustomed to roaming the coast for the most abundant runs of salmon must now "stack" three licences on their vessels in order to continue to roam the coast. With every licence "stacked" in this way, another boat leaves the fleet forever. Those that remain are being junked and sold off to be replaced by faster, more lethal boats that require fewer deckhands and less maintenance. In the spring of 1998, the consequences of the Mifflin Plan were showing up at welfare offices and battered-women's shelters from Steveston to Prince Rupert. The consequences for Canfisco were tied up to a wharf in Burrard Inlet. Fourteen seine boats – wooden classics, each a symbol of the coast's heritage, and each a tribute to this coast's great tradition of maritime architecture – were for sale. The Canfisco boats included the *Skidegate*, the *Cape May*, and the *J.H. Todd*. Some of the boats were built in the 1920s, and they were all in great shape. They were being replaced by the high-tech, low-maintenance aluminum kind. Real fish-killers.

Meanwhile, the Department of Fisheries and Oceans' sister agency, the Department of Indian Affairs, expedited the consolidation of the industry by pouring hundreds of millions of dollars into various schemes over the years designed to maintain the role of native communities as mere harvesters of fish. Much of that public money went directly to the larger fishing companies, in the form of direct federal purchases of old gillnet boats from B.C. Packers and Ocean Fisheries Ltd., which were then turned over to native communities.

At the heart of this history of exploitation and abandonment is the almost feudal condition that the coast's small fishing communities, native and non-native, must contend with as they grapple to maintain some control over the coast's natural resources, and to accrue some sustainable economic benefit from those resources.

In theory, fishing licences are held by individuals. In practice, licences are held by whoever can afford one, and their costs ($80,000 was the going price for a Skeena gillnet licence in 1997; a seine licence could fetch five times that much) continued to inflate with every fleet-reduction scheme. In theory, fishing licences are annually-renewable privileges, issued at the discretion of the Crown. In practice, licences become tradable commodities, as often as not owned by vertically-integrated companies. Licences have become speculative real estate, and as is often said about real estate in land, they ain't making any more of it. That's what "licence limitation" means.

As bizarre as it seems, in the 21st century, non-native communities along B.C.'s coast have no rights of access to the marine resources surrounding them. They have no legal authority to limit access to those resources, no role in determining who should harvest surpluses or how they should be harvested, and no say in what should be done with the raw resource. For all the dedicated and hard-working employees of Fisheries and Oceans Canada, and even the occasional well-meaning fisheries minister, it's all still pretty feudal.

In native communities, what meagre rights of access to traditional resources do exist have been won at the expense of decades of civil disobedience, poisoned relations with non-native fishermen, and lengthy criminal trials. As the 1990s wore on, tentative attempts at treaty-making were stumbling ahead – B.C. is unique in Confederation in not having got around to the job of treaty-making – holding out the promise of securing to native communities some certain resource-access rights. But every step forward was met by vitriolic anti-Indian campaigns, counselled and often funded by the big players in the fishing industry. Their rhetoric often bears a striking resemblance to the "yellow-peril" scares of the early 1900s, and to the "Japanese submarine" frights that preceded the evacuation and internment of the entire Japanese-Canadian community in the 1940s.

Just as the small community of fishermen at Namu, 6,000 years ago, were pioneering a new epoch in the history of human societies on the planet, communities all over B.C.'s coast, at the close of the 20th century, were at another crossroads in human history. Just as the early Holocene epoch marked the end of geological and ecological tumult and the stabilization of coastal habitats, the beginning of the 21st century marks an important moment in the human history of the coast. The industrial revolution in the salmon fisheries has come and gone. Conventional industrial forestry, with all its clearcuts and trashed salmon creeks, never did reach much of the coast north of Cape Caution, and at the advent of the 21th century it seems unlikely to. Some communities are considering salmon farms as an option. Kitasoo was the first community north of Cape Caution to establish an aquaculture tenure, and others are on the way. Still other communities want nothing to do with salmon farms, with their pollution of local ecosystems and the diseases they bring. At the same time, there is no single signpost, no single "right way," and no magic bullet to the many challenges facing the coast's fishing communities.

The questions are about how to emerge somehow from the ruins of the Industrial Revolution in an age of scarcity and great uncertainty. The questions are also about how to adapt in an age that will feature measurable changes in ocean productivity – some for the better, and some not – and changes in marine survival rates for salmon that may last decades. Research by the North Pacific Anadromous Fish Commission, the Scripps Institute of Oceanography and the Pacific Biological Station suggests that a cyclical curve in ocean productivity was passed in the late 1980s, and for some decades to come, some salmon runs may not be as resilient as they had been for much of the 20th century. Adapting to these changes, and choosing which paths to take, involve some difficult decisions for B.C.'s coastal communities. That's the hard part.

The easy part is that, generally speaking, the resources are still here. The great, staggering abundances are gone, but that's hardly news. In 1967, the renowned coastal storyteller Hugh McKervill was already lashing out at the way the local fishing grounds had become "monopolized by the rapacious fleet from the big city," and even then, McKervill noted that "the jocund days when Louie Hall and his crew from the village of Klemtu could scoop up 47,000 humpbacks in one set are gone forever." But forever means different things to different people. It took a mere 6,000 years for salmon to recolonize every stream and ditch this side of the Rocky Mountains after the glaciers of the Pleistocene started to melt, and whatever might be said of the tremendous hammering fisheries resources have suffered, most of the distinct genetic populations that produced those abundances are still here. In remnants, maybe, but they're still here.

Just as important is the fact that the people of Cormorant and Wiigyet and Raven are here still, too. After decades of decline and eclipse, the coast's native population has rebounded. They didn't leave when the canneries left. By 2000, about 25 per cent of the northwest coast's people were aboriginal. To a great extent, their knowledge – the old knowledge, which sustained communities for thousands of years, and the knowledge passed down in recent generations, from father to son and mother to daughter – is still with us, too.

The questions facing each coastal community at the beginning of the 21st century are about how to make a living within the natural limits of marine resources that have sustained people here ever since that egg-shaped stone went missing from somebody's tacklebox, at Namu, about 9,000 years ago. There are answers to these questions.

The questions facing each coastal community in the 2000s are about how to make a living within the natural limits of marine resources that have sustained people here

Jan and Mike Lemon putting a coho salmon into a holding tube at Letts' hatchery on the Oona River. Small hatcheries like this are slowly helping the local economy rebound. JOE SCOTT

From community to community, there are a variety of approaches emerging.

At Oona River, the Letts family are among those that have decided to tough it out. A remote Porcher Island community on Grenville Channel a couple of hours by gillnet boat south of Prince Rupert, Oona River is home to a handful of families, mostly descendants of a small group of Scottish and Scandinavian settlers who arrived there shortly after the turn of the century. At Oona River, there is a big, soft-spoken fisherman named Ralph Letts. Ralph would never be so vain as to claim such a thing, but all the same, in his own memory he has assembled more hard data about salmon populations and spawning habitat, over a vast area of channels and islands between Prince Rupert and Bella Bella, than the Department of Fisheries and Oceans could ever dream of assembling. He is not an old man. He was born in 1958.

For Ralph Letts, the future is all about those small stocks, mainly pink, coho and chum. In part,

it's about small, labour-intensive hatcheries – like the successful coho hatchery his community has built to revive the Oona's own spawning populations – deployed strategically to pump a bit of life back into near-barren spawning streams. It is also about small-scale, carefully-deployed fisheries and more diversified sources of income for local people. Even fancy terms like "ecotourism" demand a lot of plain old common sense, by Ralph's reckoning: "You've got to have fish and birds in all these little stream systems, even if it was just for tourism," Ralph observed. "People would like to walk up those creeks if there was fish spawning in them, right?"

Far up the Skeena River, in the Gitxsan communities of Gitsegukla, Gitwangak and Kispiox, there is a wholly different approach taking shape. It involves returning to the old fishing practices, the kind that worked, thousands of years before the canneries came.

By the early 1990s, the Gitxsan and Wet'suwet'en hereditary chiefs were engaged in a campaign of protracted civil disobedience that included, among its objectives, some revival of an inland commercial fishery. At the same time, the chiefs were at the forefront of the campaign to scale back the mixed-stock fisheries at the Skeena mouth that were responsible for declines of upriver steelhead, chinook and coho populations.

Because DFO had spent decades boosting the production of Babine sockeye by building artificial spawning channels – and because there were times during the sockeye run when it was impossible to "crop" the surplus in conventional rivermouth gill-net fisheries – it had become common for the Babine spawning channels to get literally "plugged up" with a surfeit of sockeye. While the hereditary chiefs had vowed to reclaim some share of the commercial wealth of Skeena sockeye, to alleviate the poverty of reserve communities, the last thing they wanted to do was lobby for greater access to the gillnet fishery downriver, or put more of their own set-gillnets in the Skeena upriver. That would only contribute to the decline of local coho, steelhead and chinook runs that were being hammered in "mixed-stock" fisheries to begin with.

"We didn't want to compound the mixed-stock fishing problem," the Gitxsan's Vince Jackson explained. "We were committed to doing things differently."

Back in 1991 – his first year as the head of the Gitxsan's fisheries operations – Jackson was already a fishing industry veteran. He'd spent years as Ocean Fisheries' netloft manager in Prince Rupert. But at this new task, Jackson was a rookie. Everybody was.

The Gitxsan started their sockeye program by reviving an old dipnet fishery at Kisgegas Canyon, on the Babine. Then came some experiments with aluminum fish traps, which seemed to scare away far more fish than they caught because aluminum poles, set in a rapid river, tend to sound a lot like a 747 taking off.

"So we started to have a lot of meetings with the elders," Jackson said. "I mean, I'd been reading the archives, so I started to ask people, 'Does anybody remember the old days? What about those weirs? What about traps?'"

The revival was a rickety business. After some tentative experiments, Jackson and his crew settled on beach-seining as a modern form of the old methods Hans Helgeson had destroyed shortly after the turn of the century. Jackson remembered the experiment's first days: "We figured we'd just throw the seine out there and see what happens. We did it at about five in the morning, because we figured that if we got up that early, there wouldn't be a whole bunch of people standing around laughing at us if it didn't work."

The Gitxsan fisheries were bitterly opposed by the Prince Rupert commercial fisheries lobby. But the Gitxsan experiments worked. Over the years, the Gitxsan's live-capture was refined and expanded, until by 1997, it was one of the most tightly controlled, productive and cost-efficient fisheries on B.C.'s coast. The fishery provides crucial stock-composition and run-timing data for DFO's fisheries managers. It provides a sorely-needed source of income for local native families. It harvests only known surpluses. It's a fishery that harvests to a precise number of fish – unlike the guesswork involved in almost all other fisheries – and it only kills fish from the species and the stocks it's intended to kill.

Meanwhile, downriver, Prince Rupert gillnetters Fred and Linda Hawkshaw were working on their own solutions to the mixed-stock problem, and in the process they ended up with a solution to the small-boat salmon fisherman's biggest challenge in the 1900s – getting decent prices for fish.

Absurd market distortions in the salmon economy, caused mainly by the rapid growth of farmed salmon, had meant that the price fishermen could command for wild salmon, in the late 1990s, was about a third what it was a decade before. This is true for all species of salmon, and for every fleet sector – seine, gillnet and troll. Prince Rupert gillnetters found themselves facing prices as low as 90 cents a pound for their sockeye in 1997, and while sockeye, chinook and coho prices can fluctuate wildly, all the long-term forecasts for salmon prices are grim. The usual solution to low prices is to simply invest in more lethal gear, and catch more fish – the classic treadmill of overcapitalization that so often results in overfishing and fisheries collapses. To make matters worse, Skeena gillnetters were getting squeezed into fewer fishing openings because of the need to conserve coho. The Hawkshaws were hurting, like everybody else in the gillnet fleet.

But the Hawkshaws had a simple idea. For one, a gillnet doesn't have to "gill" the fish, if the mesh size is small enough. Instead of pulling up dead fish that have suffocated in gillnets, a smaller mesh size could ensnare the fish by the maxillary – a sockeye's "jawbone." What that allows is a couple of things. The first is that you get fish that are still alive. You have to haul your net more frequently, and you have to be fussy about things, but the fish can be bled, cleaned and iced with as much care as the most fastidious troller might take. This means you end up with a product of far higher quality, and by directly marketing your fish – rather than selling it to one of the coast's big fishing companies, which stuff salmon into cans – you can command a premium price for the product.

The second thing is that if you happen to entangle a steelhead or a coho, you can release the "non-target" fish live and unharmed.

That was the theory, anyway. In 1997, with the help of Ecotrust Canada, a scientific permit from DFO, and some assistance from sceptical officials with the B.C. Ministry of Agriculture, Fisheries and Food, Fred and Linda Hawkshaw proved that their theory worked. In their first experiments, only one of five coho that became entangled in the Hawkshaw's "jawnet" died, and it was a "jack" – a precocious male. Only one of 17 steelhead died in the net – an undersized fish that had the bad luck of being the last fish out of a haul of 57 in one set of the net. Except for what the seals killed, that was it, as far as mortalities go. The Hawkshaws caught a total of 680 sockeye. Rather than 90 cents a pound, the Hawkshaws ended up making between $3.60 and $3.90 a pound.

On the Nass River, the Nisga'a Tribal Council has been pioneering a different kind of fishing-gear technology that is completely new to B.C.'s coast. Since the late 1980s, the Nisga'a have been operating two sets of fishwheels – one at a lower river site, at Grease Harbour, and the other at the upriver Nisga'a village of Gitwinksihlkw. Fishwheels replicate the main characteristics of the traditional weir-and-trap fisheries of the coast: they're terminal, selective, live-capture, and produce the most precise results. What makes wheels different than traditional terminal

Fishwheel on the Nass River used to measure salmon runs. This fishwheel was designed in what became part of an award-winning salmon study.
GARY FIEGEHEN

technologies is that they spin, like miniature ferris wheels, with sloping seats. Fish swimming upriver are scooped up in the "seats" of the wheel, which spin with the current of the river. Once caught, they slide off the wheel into live pens.

The Nass River fishwheels are part of a fisheries program that integrates a variety of functions, including tagging, biological sampling, tag recapture, harvest of surpluses, secondary tagging and secondary tagging recapture. The system provides immediate and reliable run-timing data and run-strength estimates. Among the successes of the Nisga'a fisheries program is that in 1992, for the first time ever, Fisheries and Oceans scientists could say something intelligent when they were asked about Nass River steelhead. Before then, Fisheries and Oceans officials had absolutely no information about Nass steelhead. After 1992, when the Nisga'a fishwheels allowed for a comprehensive monitoring program, Fisheries and Oceans was provided with better information about steelhead on the Nass than any information base the department maintained on steelhead for any other river system in British Columbia.

By 1998, the pioneering work of the Gitxsan fishermen, the Hawkshaws, and the Nisga'a had blazed a trail for Fisheries and Oceans

By 1998, the pioneering work of the Gitxsan fishermen, the Hawkshaws, and the Nisga'a had blazed a trail for Fisheries and Oceans. In 1998, Fisheries Minister David Anderson declared that "selective fisheries management" would become the "cornerstone" of salmon management on Canada's west coast. The days of focusing all of the fleet's fishing effort in mixed-stock fishing were finally coming to an end.

The Nisga'a were also busy through the 1990s pioneering something else. In 1999, more than a century after the first Nisga'a Land Committee was formed, the Nisga'a concluded the first Canadian treaty to be negotiated west of the Rocky Mountains. In an element of the deal that provoked uproars of outrage from the coast's fishing companies, the Nisga'a had wrested from federal negotiators a degree of security in tenure to their own traditional marine resources. In the treaty's fisheries component, about $11-million is set aside to allow the Nisga'a to purchase fishboats, and the Nisga'a communities are guaranteed the equivalent of about 120,000 sockeye a year, when the runs are healthy. In a side agreement, the Nisga'a are guaranteed the chance to catch more sockeye, and sell them if they choose, according to a formula that still guarantees the coastal commercial fishing industry the lion's share of the Nass River's harvestable salmon surplus. The deal denies the Nisga'a the opportunity to establish their own major fishplants for at least 12 years after the signing of a treaty. Still, the Nisga'a are planning to build their own fish processing facilities when that day comes. In some years, the Nisga'a sockeye allocation could reach 28 per cent of whatever is left over after spawning-escapement goals are met, after the Alaskan fleet takes its share, and after "incidental harvests" from fisheries in Canadian waters are deducted.

Whatever might be said of the content of the Nisga'a fisheries component, its function is to apply the brakes, at least with respect to Nass River salmon, on all those trends that have combined over the years to remove the wealth of the coast's fisheries resources from the communities of the coast. The treaty's fisheries component establishes what fisheries economists have long understood as a necessary precondition for the existence of "sustainable" fisheries: the presence of an economically viable fishery conducted upon particular stocks of fish, the health and abundance of which local fishing communities have a direct economic interest in maintaining. The fishing management plans anticipated by the Nisga'a envision a mix of gear types, of "public" and "private" enterprise, of community benefit and individual entrepreneurship. The deal allows some certainty, for the first time since the canneries came, that a degree of the wealth of the fishery, formerly subject to export, will remain in the region. It is a modest arrangement, but it still provides more constitutionally-enforceable security of tenure in the salmon fisheries than any other B.C. coastal community, native or non-native, has managed to secure for itself.

Only one other community comes close. It's Bella Bella, the principal village of the Heiltsuk. On a trip by boat from the Fraser to the Nass, Bella Bella, with about 1,500 residents, is now the largest community on the mainland coast. It is the home of the descendants of the people of Namu.

Like most other First Nations in British Columbia, the Heiltsuk were engaged in the elaborate, tripartite treaty-making process that began trundling across B.C.'s landscape after the B.C. Treaty Commission opened its doors in 1993. But in the absence of treaties in B.C., it has been left up to the Supreme Court of Canada to determine the scope and content of aboriginal fishing rights. And in the case of William and Donald Gladstone of Bella Bella, who were charged in 1988 with violating Section 20 (3) of the Pacific herring fishery regulations of the Fisheries Act, the Supreme Court decided, almost a decade after the charges were laid, that the Heiltsuk were perfectly entitled to sell spawn-on-kelp. That's what the Gladstones were doing when they were charged. The judges ruled that because such sales were consistent with the distinctive customs of the Heiltsuk people, the Heiltsuk were entitled to continue in their traditions in a contemporary manner. The legal challenge was an arduous, costly and contentious way to establish a right to involvement in a commercial fishery. But it worked.

What it meant, apart from all the intriguing implications that lawyers and historians like to talk about, was that in the spring of 1998, dozens of Heiltsuk families were scooting around the channels and inlets of Heiltsuk traditional fishing grounds, rushing to and from places like Stryker Bay and Cultus Point, engaging in a modern version of an ancient fishery that involves fooling herring into spawning on fronds of kelp strung from ropes affixed to floating logs. Another way of doing it is to harvest a huge school of herring that is about

to spawn and release the fish into a closed pond of suspended kelp. The result is a Heiltsuk delicacy, which also happens to be a popular Japanese delicacy. It's known as spawn-on-kelp, and sometimes it's called roe-on-kelp. It looks a little bit like a ham sandwich, except with a sticky mass of herring eggs instead of bread and a thin slice of kelp instead of ham. Depending on the quality, it can fetch a fisherman up to $30 a pound. It can be several months after the close of the fishery before the fisherman finally learns how much his product is worth – it depends on the negotiated price formula, the thickness of the spawn, its texture, the quality of the kelp, how well the product was brined, the value of the Japanese yen against the Canadian dollar, and a host of other factors, including a tremendous application of skill and a lot of old-fashioned luck. But a particularly busy Heiltsuk fishing family, in 1998, stood to earn more than $50,000 for their efforts.

It was in the middle of all of this frenzied activity in 1998 that John Bolton, who was then the 43-year-old Heiltsuk fisheries manager, sat behind his desk in the basement of the Bella Bella band office and tried to gather his thoughts. It had been a busy week. The Heiltsuk fish to strict quotas, and the way the landings were tallying up, the quota was expected to be reached any moment. People were always hopeful about the price, and the quality, he said. But people yearned for it, too, for themselves. They ate a lot of what they caught. Bolton squinted at the ceiling and tried to guess how much his own family would put away for themselves. Between him and his wife Sheila, John Jr. and his daughters Angeline and Marina, and then there's friends and guests – Bolton was counting on his fingers now – "I'd say 2,500 pounds," he said. "Yeah, about that. Just for the people in my house."

Heiltsuk families were...engaging in a modern version of an ancient fishery that involves fooling herring into spawning on fronds of kelp strung from ropes affixed to floating logs

Because of the Gladstone decision, as the Supreme Court decision had come to be known, the Heiltsuk were fishing to a quota in 1998 of about 96,000 pounds, or the equivalent of six commercial spawn-on-kelp licences. But unlike single commercial licences, held by individuals, the band-owned licences allowed the community to issue 227 separate permits for spawn-on-kelp in 1998. There were problems figuring out how permits should be issued – how many, and to whom, exactly, and what kind of priorities to set. But things were sorting themselves out. And that's just spawn-on-kelp.

The Heiltsuk First Nation also owns six salmon gillnet licences and a salmon seine licence, and in some years, the band leases seine and gillnet licences to participate directly in the conventional herring roe fishery. There are three band-owned rockfish licences, three sea-urchin licences, and a sea-cucumber licence. The band also holds three commercial clam-fishing permits, each with an annual quota of 250,000 pounds. With prices as high as $2.25 a pound, paid to the harvester, there

was more money in clams in 1997 than there was in sockeye, and 30 band members busied themselves digging clams for the season. Band-owned licences are leased to band members, on terms set by the community, and the lease fees offset the costs of the Heiltsuk fisheries program, which includes monitoring and patrols, fish and stream assessment and a variety of other functions. And then there are individual band members who own a variety of commercial fishing licences for salmon, rockfish, prawn and other species, so it ends up being a healthy, mixed fishing economy. And that's just the harvesting side.

Down at McLoughlin Bay, long after sunset, Alvin Dixon, the 60-year-old manager of the community-owned Bella Bella fishplant, was waiting for word about the last spawn-on-kelp deliveries of the day. The *Cowichan* and the *Back Eddy* were unloading the day's catch down at the dock, but there were still more boats to come in. A voice crackled on a VHF radio somewhere and a small forklift was roaring around outside Dixon's window, rearranging stacks of purple and blue fish totes. Alvin Dixon sat behind his desk and leaned back in his chair. He was tired.

It was shaping up to be a pretty good season, Dixon reckoned. The product he'd seen so far showed some real quality. It was too early to say anything much about prices, but at least the quality was there. And it all meant work for a core group of about 15 plant workers who'd just finished packing the bulk of the year's clam harvest before the spawn-on-kelp fishery began. Apart from the spawn-on-kelp processing, there were 250 tons of herring roe to process, and probably some more clams to move through, and that would mean work for the crews right through, almost to the salmon season. While it didn't look like much, the operation Dixon was running had become the largest fishplant on the mainland coast between Vancouver and Prince Rupert.

For five years, Dixon had been chairman and chief executive officer of B.C.'s Native Fishing Association. For three years, he'd served as executive director of the Native Brotherhood of B.C., and for 10 years, between 1983 and 1993, Dixon worked as the coordinator of native ministries for the United Church of Canada. And now here he was, after all these years, back home, working as the fish plant's first native manager.

There is hope for the coast's fishing communities, Dixon said.

"You're starting to see people coming up in the community who have the business sense, and the drive to do well," he said. "And there's even the sports fishery. I don't see any reason why we couldn't be getting into that here. There's Milbanke Sound, and Hakai Pass, and they're right here in our traditional territory."

And there was a lot more value that could be added to the fish the Heiltsuk people were already harvesting, he said. There was specialty marketing that hadn't been tapped, and custom processing, and smoked product. A bit of investment in upgrading the plant's cold-storage capability would make the world of difference, he reckoned, and there were species that hadn't even been looked at

that held promise, like seaweed, crab, gooseneck barnacles, and mussels.

"But it's a lot of hard work," Dixon said. And right about then, near the end of a long and tiring day, a lot of hard work wasn't what Dixon wanted to be thinking about too much. He laughed.

Dixon had known hard work. Like so many people of his generation, Dixon grew up in the canneries. It was what put him through school. Following Cecil Reid, a former band chief, Dixon was the second Heiltsuk person in history to earn a university degree.

He started working when he was 14, carrying heavy trays of fillets from a processing line to a freezer, hour in and hour out. When he was 15, he was running a Birdseye freezer operation, by himself, for $1.80 an hour. He was one of the highest paid Indians in the whole place.

It was at Namu.

REFERENCES

Berringer, P. A. 1982. "Northwest Coast Traditional Salmon Fisheries: Systems of Resource Utilization," Masters Thesis. British Columbia: Faculty of Graduate Studies, University of British Columbia.

British Columbia Ministry of Fisheries. 1999. "Review of the New Arrangements under the Pacific Salmon Treaty."

Cannon, A. 1991. "The Economic Prehistory of Namu." Burnaby, B.C.: Department of Archaeology, Simon Fraser University. Publication # 19.

Carlson, R. 1992. "The Native Fishery in British Columbia: The archaeological evidence." Unpublished paper.

Chisholm, Brian. 1986. "Reconstruction of Prehistoric Diet in British Columbia using Stable-carbon Isotope analyses." Doctoral thesis in archaeology. Burnaby, B.C.: Simon Fraser University.

Chisholm, B., S. Nelson, D. Erle, and H. P. Schwarcz. 1983. "Marine and Terrestrial Protein in Prehistoric Diets in the British Columbia Coast," *Current Anthropology* 24, No.3.

Department of Fisheries and Oceans. 1999. Miscellaneous Pacific Salmon Treaty background documents.

Department of Fisheries and Oceans. 1998. "Coho Backgrounder."

Ellis, D. 1996. *Net Loss: The Salmon Netcage Industry in British Columbia*. Vancouver, B.C.: David Suzuki Foundation.

Galaugher, P. and L. Wood, eds. 1998. "Speaking for the Salmon." Workshop Proceedings. Aboriginal Fisheries Commission. Burnaby, B.C.: Continuing Studies, Simon Fraser University.

Gislason, G., E. Lam, and M. Mohan. 1996. "Fishing For Answers: Coastal Communities and the B.C. Salmon Fishery." Final Report. B.C. Job Protection Commission. ARA Consulting Group, Inc.

Harris, C. 1977. *The Resettlement of British Columbia: Essays on Colonialism and Geographical Change*. Vancouver, B.C.: University of British Columbia Press.

Hewes, G.W. 1973. "Indian fisheries Productivity in Pre-Contact Times in the Pacific Salmon Area." Northwest Anthropological Research Notes 7, No.2.

Holtby, L.B. and B. Finegan. 1998. "A biological assessment of the coho salmon of the Skeena River, British Columbia, and recommendations for fisheries in 1998." Salmon Subcommittee Working Paper S9712. Stock Assessment Division, Science Branch, Department of Fisheries and Oceans.

Lamb, W. K. 1970. *The Journals and Letters of Sir Alexander Mackenzie*. Toronto: MacMillan and Company.

Lazenby, R. and P. McCormack. 1985. "Salmon and Malnutrition on the Northwest Coast" *Current Anthropology* 26, No.3.

Lillard, C. 1989. *The Ghostland People: A Documentary History of the Queen Charlotte Islands*. Sono Nis Press.

McKervill, H. W. 1967. *The Salmon People*. Sidney, B.C.: Gray's Publishing Ltd.

Mooney, J. 1910. "Population." *Bureau of American Ethnology* Bulletin 30.

Muszynski, A. 1996. *Cheap Wage Labour: Race and Gender in the Fisheries of British Columbia*. McGill/Queen's University Press.

Newell, D., ed. 1989. *The Development of the Pacific Salmon Canning Industry: A Grown Man's Game*. McGill/Queen's University Press.

Pomeroy, J.A. "Stone Fish Traps of the Bella Bella Region," *Current Research Reports*. R.L. Carlson, ed., Department of Archaeology, Simon Fraser University. Publication No.3:165-173.

Rutherford, D. and C. Wood. 2000. "Trends in Abundance and Pre-Season 2000 Stock Size Forecasts for major Sockeye, Pink and Chum Salmon Stocks in the Central Coast, and Selected Salmon Stocks in Northern British Columbia." PSARC Report, 2000.

Slaney, T., K. Hyatt, T.G. Northcote, and R.J. Fielden. 1996. "Status of Anadromous Salmon and Trout in British Columbia and the Yukon" *Fisheries* 21:10.

Steltzer, U. and C. Kerr. 1982. *Coast of Many Faces. Vancouver*, B.C.: Douglas and McIntyre.

Suttles, W. and K. Ames. 1997. "Pre-European History," *The Rain Forests of Home*. Peter K. Schoonmaker, Bettina Von Hagen, and Edward C. Wolf, eds. Washington, D.C: Ecotrust/Interrain, Island Press.

Williams, J. 1996. High Slack: *Waddington's Gold Road and the Bute Inlet Massacre of 1864*. Transmontanus/New Star.

Williams, J.T., H. Helgeson, et al. 1905. "Thirty-Eighth Annual Report of the Department of Marine and Fisheries." Ottawa. 206-211.

Wood, A. 2000. "State of Salmon Conservation in the Central Coast Area" Report to the Pacific Fisheries Resource Conservation Council.

MAP 2.1 Salmon and steelhead status by watershed

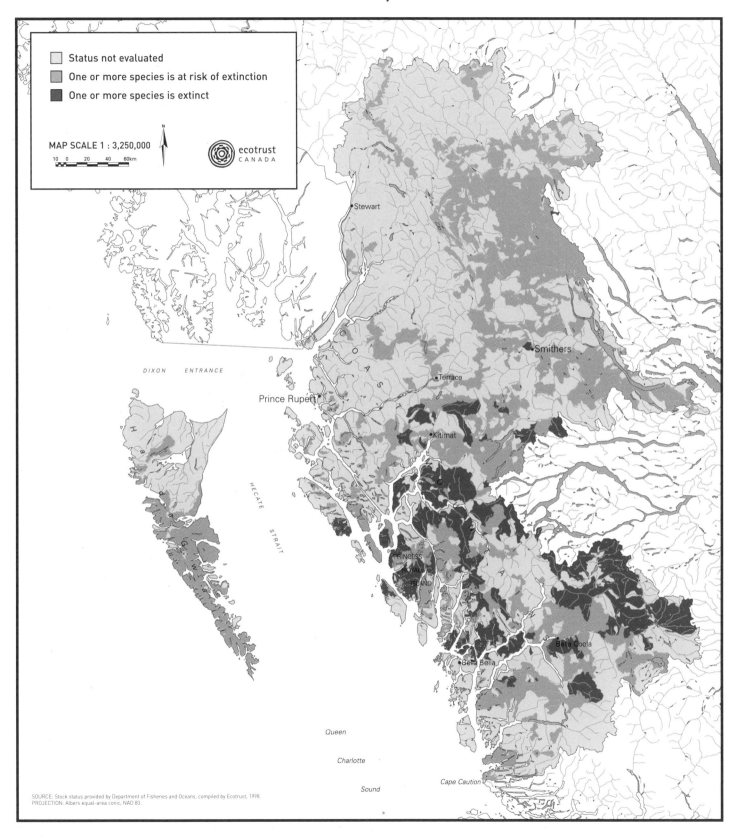

Status not evaluated

One or more species is at risk of extinction

One or more species is extinct

MAP SCALE 1 : 3,250,000

10 0   20   40   60km

N

ecotrust
CANADA

DIXON   ENTRANCE

Stewart

Smithers

Terrace

Prince Rupert

Kitimat

HECATE

STRAIT

PRINCESS
ROYAL
ISLAND

Bella Coola

Bella Bella

Queen

Charlotte

Sound

Cape Caution

SOURCE: Stock status provided by Department of Fisheries and Oceans, compiled by Ecotrust, 1998.
PROJECTION: Albers equal-area conic, NAD 83.

MAP 2.2a Historic distribution of canneries

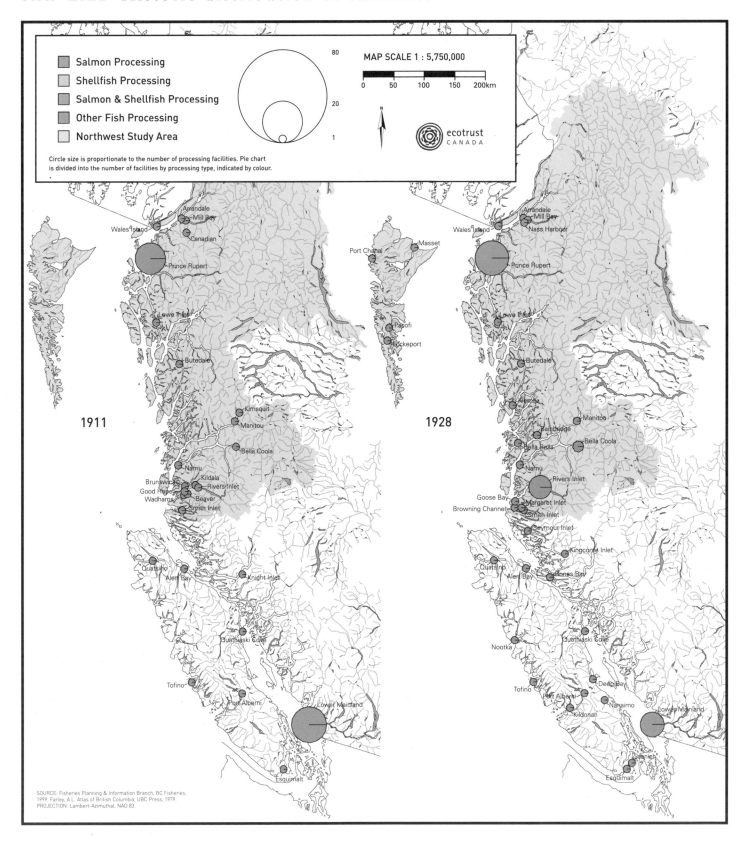

Salmon Processing

Shellfish Processing

Salmon & Shellfish Processing

Other Fish Processing

Northwest Study Area

Circle size is proportionate to the number of processing facilities. Pie chart
is divided into the number of facilities by processing type, indicated by colour.

MAP SCALE 1 : 5,750,000

0   50   100   150   200km

ecotrust
CANADA

1911

Arrandale
Mill Bay
Wales Island
Canadian
Prince Rupert
Lowe Inlet
Butedale
Kimsquit
Manitou
Bella Coola
Namu
Kildala
Brunswick
Good Hope
Wadhams
Beaver
Rivers Inlet
Smith Inlet
Quatsino
Alert Bay
Knight Inlet
Quathiaski Cove
Tofino
Port Alberni
Lower Mainland
Esquimalt

Port Chanal
Masset
Pacofi
Lockeport

1928

Arrandale
Mill Bay
Wales Island
Nass Harbour
Prince Rupert
Lowe Inlet
Butedale
Klemtu
Manitou
Bainbridge
Bella Bella
Bella Coola
Namu
Rivers Inlet
Goose Bay
Margaret Inlet
Browning Channel
Smith Inlet
Seymour Inlet
Kingcome Inlet
Quatsino
Alert Bay
Bones Bay
Quathiaski Cove
Nootka
Deep Bay
Tofino
Port Alberni
Nanaimo
Kildonan
Saanich
Esquimalt
Lower Mainland

SOURCE: Fisheries Planning & Information Branch, BC Fisheries,
1999. Farley, A.L. Atlas of British Columbia, UBC Press, 1979.
PROJECTION: Lambert-Azimuthal, NAD 83.

MAP 2.2b Historic distribution of canneries

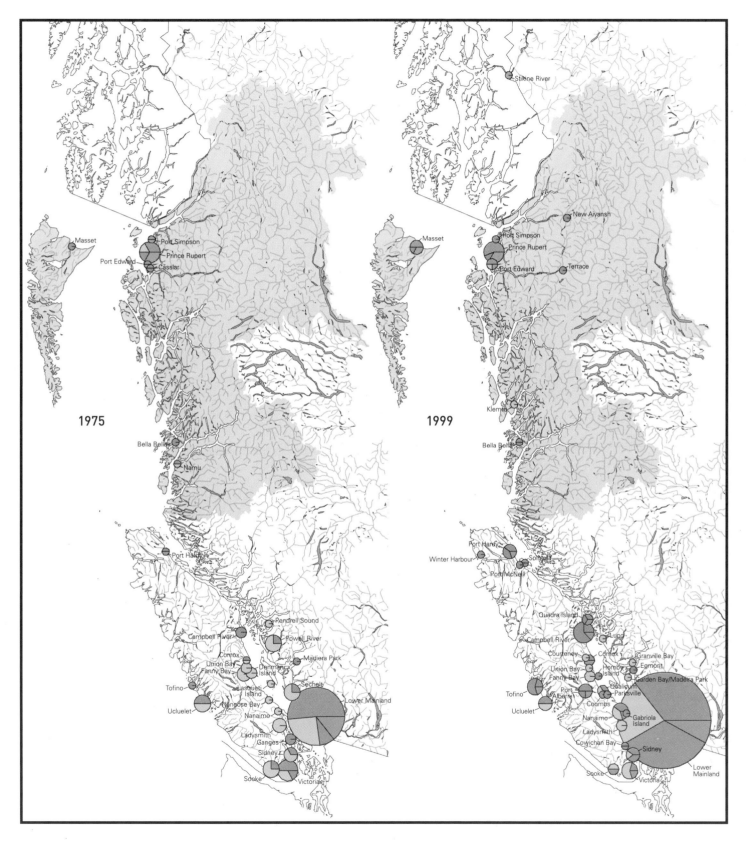

1975

1999

Chapter	# The Lands
3	*By Ben Parfitt*

IN THE CORNER OF A CAFE IN AN OLD WOOD-FRAME BUILDING AT THE NORTH PACIFIC CANNERY Village Museum stands a story pole carved by Nisga'a carver Murphy Stanley. The raised figure of a frog sits atop, peering down at a stern looking Nisga'a man whose face is divided in two by a sharp red line that cuts down the forehead, the bridge of the nose, the upper and lower lips, and finally the chin. The pole tells the story of the divided man. One day, two argumentative men in the Nisga'a frog clan were sucked into one body. There they spent the rest of their lives, forced to sort out their differences inside the same skin. That is what the spirits decided. That is how it would be.

It is a cool, grey, rainy May morning at the old cannery outside Port Edward near the coastal community of Prince Rupert. I am sitting in the cafe with its former manager, Tony Duggleby, and as I listen to Duggleby's story about the big crushing the interests of the small, I can't help wonder what this part of the world would look like if a few bodies were transported into one. What would the surrounding forest look like, what would the activities of the people who live off the fruits of that forest resemble if some of the more stubborn of them were forced to march through life together? What would have to change so that they could inhabit the same body without cutting off their own limbs?

As I enter the cafe, Duggleby is fishing around inside a power box in the corner opposite the story pole. A few shards of plastic-coated, copper wiring lie discarded on a tabletop beside a screwdriver, a pair of pliers, and a half-filled cup of coffee. For a while, Duggleby continues fiddling with the wiring as he tells his story. But pretty soon he's given up multi-tasking. His friend and co-worker Dwayne Jackson arrives from the kitchen with freshly brewed coffee and warm sticky buns. By this time, I've learned that Duggleby left a longstanding job with the Canadian National Railway

Throughout the forests of the coast there is historical evidence of a rich, once thriving culture. "Culturally modified trees" such as this were tested by First Nations hundreds of years ago for strength and health. GARY FIEGEHEN

The Skeena Cellulose pulp mill is on the decline and slowly approaching bankruptcy. It is Prince Rupert's largest employer. ALEX ROSE

"I ask questions. I find out things. You follow where the conversation leads and you learn. Here in Rupert there's lots of logs in booms and on barges. And almost all of that wood ends up being shipped out of here. When you hear about a German guy coming to town, buying one log out of a boom and shipping it back to Germany for use in instrument wood you know that's something different. And if you're like me you say, 'Now *that's* interesting.'"

It didn't take Duggleby long to learn that there was immense value in certain trees. He came to learn, for example, that Jean Larrivee, a Vancouver-based guitar maker of international renown, had flown to Rupert where he paid $10,000 for a single 25-foot-long, 4-foot-diameter Sitka spruce log. He learned about the qualities of logs that made for good guitars. He learned about the physical properties of logs, how they had to be cut in just the right way to create the wood pieces for the guitar's most important part – the top. And he slowly worked his way into the business of finding the logs and learning to make those all-important cuts himself – a demanding task.

in 1985 rather than be transferred from Rupert to Smithers or Prince George, more than 600 kilometres to the east down the Yellowhead Highway.

For Duggleby and many others, Rupert is a hard place to leave. They stay despite the fact that after a $350-million taxpayer bailout the city's biggest employer, the Skeena Cellulose pulp mill, is still only a market downturn away from potential bankruptcy. They stay despite the fact that a once-strong fishing industry has been decimated by overfishing and the concentration of fishing licences in the hands of distant corporate interests. And they stay despite the fact that the local tourism sector took a big hit in the summer of 1997, when B.C. fishermen vented their anger at their Alaskan counterparts by engaging in a high-profile blockade of an Alaskan ferry attempting to leave Rupert's port. This is home. This is where their families live and have lived, in some cases for three generations, since the town's founding in 1911. They stay put.

Duggleby is a survivor whose insatiable curiosity has stood him in good stead. As the rain pelts down on the cafe's roof and the outside boardwalk linking the cannery's many buildings together, Duggleby tells a story about how his inquisitive nature carried him from the railway business into a contract with Gibson Guitars in distant Bozeman, Montana.

"Have you ever taken a hatchet to a two-by-four?" Duggleby asked. "If you have, you know that it usually doesn't split in a straight line." This has to do with the way lumber is processed and the way that a sawyer's blade cuts across the natural grains in a log. If you look at the end of a two-by-four, you see curving lines that cut across and exit the end at different points. The face of the board is different, but somewhat the same. On the face, you find longer, straighter, lines. But even these lines do not run cleanly from one end of the board to the other. Some of the lines that start at the top exit the board before they reach the bottom. If you try to split such a board the break won't be clean. It will follow the natural grains in the wood. Hidden inside the wood is also a third grain called a medullary ray. These rays are dark, short grains that run at 90-degree angles between the longitudinal grains. They can be seen in varying numbers depending on how a log is broken down into pieces. Cut it wrong and you'll see few if any of these rays.

All of which is important if you want to make high-value wooden products such as blanks, which are the thin boards used by instrument makers to fashion guitar tops. Duggleby grabs some waste paper and a pen and, with the aid of a few quick diagrams, explains how to extract gold from a Sitka spruce log. The best blanks have these characteristics: the ring grains on the thin ends of the blanks run parallel to each other and vertical to the face. On the blank's face, the longitudinal grains run the full length of the 24-inch long piece. If the grains on the end and top are perfectly straight and do not enter or exit the board at odd angles, the face will be filled with lots of medullary rays. The critically important first step in making a world-class guitar will be complete. "The person cutting the blanks really determines the value of the guitar," Duggleby said, as he puts his pen down. "If he's two or three degrees off, it's a $200 or $300 drugstore guitar. If he's really spot on 90 degrees, some of the guitars made from that wood will sell as high as $5,000."

Over the years, Duggleby purchased a small band saw. His talent cutting blanks grew. He became good enough at it to become a supplier to Gibson Guitars. At one point in 1989, he supplied 600 blanks a month to the guitar-maker at an agreed on price of US$12 per unit or US$7,200 a month before expenses. But for a variety of reasons, including intransigence on the part of the lead government agency charged with overseeing British Columbia's publicly owned forests, Duggleby is out of the woodworking business and into the tourism trade.

It is the next part of this story that has me looking more and more at the story pole. As I stare at the man with the split face, I try to picture somebody from the Ministry of Forests or the senior manager of one of the region's bigger forest companies forced to inhabit the same body with a small businessman such as Duggleby. What would emerge from this forced union? Would the two men war with each other, ripping their shared body in two? Or would they learn to accommodate each other? And if so, how?

On the surface, Duggleby's wants seem comically simple. In a province where more than 200,000 hectares of forest are clearcut annually, Duggleby wants three to five good trees per year. That's it. "I could have myself and two other families living off of that comfortably. And that's only 15 to 30 cubic metres. That's all we would need. And that would support three families in very good style – $3,000 to $4,000 per family per month."

The problem is he can't get the wood.

For five years beginning in 1985, Duggleby hounded the local Ministry of Forests (MoF) offices to let him cut down this or that particular tree. These types of timber sales are known as cash sales, and they used to be fairly common. Cash sales work this way. You walk into an area of Crown forest (in B.C. about 94 per cent of the forest is publicly owned). You find a tree suitable to your needs. You mark it, and then return to the district MoF offices to negotiate its sale. Sounds simple enough. But in Duggleby's experience, MoF resistance to the sales was evident almost from the word go. "The problem is it would take a guy two man-days of work to go to the tree, then process it for sale," Duggleby said.

It wasn't long before Duggleby found himself unable to secure cash sales and forced, instead, to bid on logging thousands of trees just to get the few spruce that were of a high enough quality to turn into guitar tops. At the government's urging, he became a participant in the ministry's Small Business Forest Enterprise Program. On paper, this unfortunately named program is supposed to serve the interests of contract loggers as well as small businesses involved in the production of higher-value wood products. Allotments of timber in varying volumes are auctioned through one of two sales categories. The first category is meant to assist contract loggers to get access to wood. Under this category a volume of timber is put up for sale, the ministry sets a minimum price to be paid for the wood, and interested parties bid over and above the minimum price with the highest bid carrying the day. The second category is referred to as a "bid proposal." Under these sales, the ministry again puts a volume

The top ten companies directly control more than 58 per cent of the trees logged each year in the province's publicly-owned forests

of timber up for sale. It then entertains bids from companies who want to process that timber into value-added wood products. Bids are assessed on the basis of the jobs that will be created, the type of product manufactured, and the social and economic benefits that accrue from the sale at the district or provincial level.

One thing relating to the distribution of wealth tends, however, to undermine the success of the small business program. The majority of timber logged outside of the program is controlled directly by a relatively small number of forest companies who also own most of the commodity sawmills and pulp mills in the province. The top 10 companies, for example, directly control more than 58 per cent of the trees logged each year in the province's publicly owned forests.[1] The Ministry of Forests determines the price paid for this wood, under the direction of the provincial government. It is an administered pricing system, not immediately responsive to prices paid in the open market, and often below the prices paid in more competitive settings, such as small business program timber sales.

Because the larger companies control so much timber, and because they pay less for that timber than others who rely on the open market for log supplies, they are in a position to outbid smaller companies who turn to the small business program for wood. The big companies are not, strictly speaking, allowed to participate in the program. But a common practice is for them to join with a logging contractor who acts as a surrogate bidder. Working together, the two agree on a bid. The contractor gets paid a set price in return for the wood going to the company backing him. All of which means that if you happen to be somebody like Duggleby you must be prepared to pay a prohibitively high price for a lot of wood you may not want just to ensure that it does not fall into the hands of one of the major companies.

In the North Coast forest district that takes in Prince Rupert and environs, the average volume of timber sold under the small business program between 1996 and 1998 was more than 13,000 cubic metres.[2] These were the kind of timber sales Duggleby bid on. Only a tiny fraction of the wood in such sales – about 0.2 per cent – was actually suitable for guitar-top making. But if Duggleby wanted that wood, he had to absorb all the financial risk of logging and marketing the rest of it.

"Ten thousand cubic metres was my first sale," Duggleby recalled. "I had to do it. I'd log off the patch, I figured, sell off everything I didn't want, and keep the five or ten trees that I wanted. My next sale was for 5,000 cubic metres, and then I went into Kemano and cleaned up between 6,500 and 7,000 cubic metres of blowdown wood, all nice big valley-bottom spruce. The problem was that I ended up doing less and less guitar tops because I had to pay so much attention to logging. To this day, if they let me go out and cut one tree down, I'd be a happy camper."

Just to get the right to log his first "small" timber sale, Duggleby had to pay a $16,000 deposit to the ministry. Then there was the cost of the logging equipment itself, about $30,000. And that was for boat logging, a relatively cheap form of logging that is virtually unheard of today (the ministry claims this logging method is environmentally insensitive and does not comply with B.C.'s Forest Practices Code). Which is to say that if you want to log in the small business program these days you'd better be prepared to log a lot of wood and you'd better have a lot of money up front. Furthermore, you'll have to do so on an uneven playing field. If you're like Duggleby and don't have many secured assets, your deposit must be in cash. If, on the other hand, you're a major forest company with lots of assets, your deposit may be nothing more than a letter from the bank guaranteeing that if the deposit is called in the bank will pay it.

And all of this is beside the point anyway. As Duggleby said, he's *not interested* in logging. He wants to be a guitar-top maker. It would be easy to conclude from all of this that the big companies and the ministry are wittingly or unwittingly crushing the interests of the small. But as enticing as the big-is-bad, small-is-good argument is, it doesn't hold true in today's world. The fact is that there are many, many value-added enterprises across British Columbia and around the world that aren't in the business of logging or, for that matter, the business of log processing. These businesses don't want to spread their finite finances across a range of activities that begin with logging, proceed to primary processing and end with the creation of high-value wood products. What they want is delivery of a commodity – be it a log or a board – which can then be turned into a higher-value product. Given this, it's perfectly reasonable to expect that there will be companies (some big, some small) who will act as a bridge between the forest and the secondary or value-added wood processors. What is not reasonable or desirable from the perspective of a sound environment, sound economy and sound society, is to have a privileged few companies controlling almost all of a publicly-owned resource, and turning that resource into billions of feet of cheap commodity lumber and mountains of market pulp.

As respected sociologist and author of *Logging the Globe* Patricia Marchak once observed: "A lot of our problem is that we build and build the same damn thing. And so we've got massive overcapacity. There isn't something intrinsically wrong with the forest industry, it seems to me, any more intrinsically wrong than a salmon-fishing industry or a cod-fishing industry or anything else. It's the *scale* on which it has been done that is destroying the whole thing."[3]

To inhabit the same space, the small businessman must accept that there is a role and a place for bigger companies. Conversely, the big businessman must learn that too much of one thing forecloses on future options and weakens the body. (Much the same could be said of governments who serve the interests of the big before the small.) To co-exist and live within means requires accepting limits and then doing the most you can with what's left.

Unfortunately, the scale that Marchak decries remains rooted in place. The interests of the big usurp the interests of the small, to the detriment of indigenous and non-indigenous communities throughout B.C.

Before turning to examples of how things might be done differently, let's take some time to look at the northwest coastal region of B.C. The northwest coast is a vast region, home to some of the world's last remaining temperate rainforests and adjacent transition forests that bridge the gap between the wetter, cooler coastal forest and the drier, hotter interior forest. Most of the economic spin-offs associated with the clearcutting of this region's forests accrue to large, integrated forest companies whose headquarters and major processing facilities are located in the southern reaches of the coast, roughly south of a line between Campbell River on Vancouver Island's east coast and Powell River, across the Strait of Georgia on B.C.'s mainland coast.

There are 11 pulp and paper facilities on B.C.'s coast. The northernmost mill is in Prince Rupert, the southernmost on the Fraser River in New Westminster. The pulp and paper sector is the biggest consumer of wood fibre worldwide, and B.C. is no exception. Each year, B.C.'s coastal pulp industry consumes nearly 20 million cubic metres of wood fibre.[4] Much of that fibre comes from logs

Freshly milled two-by-fours destined for Los Angeles.
GARY FIEGEHEN

More than half of all materials produced at sawmills end up at pulp and paper mills like the Skeena Cellulose pulpmill in Prince Rupert.
GARY FIEGEHEN

In 1999, the Ministry of Forests estimated that fully 56 per cent of the material entering sawmills ended up not as lumber but as chips, sawdust and shavings

that are chipped expressly for pulp production. The rest of the fibre comes from sawmills. When sawmills cut round logs into boards, significant portions of the logs cannot be turned into lumber. In 1999, the Ministry of Forests estimated that fully 56 per cent of the material entering sawmills ended up not as lumber but as chips, sawdust and shavings. Almost all of that material later wound up in the province's pulp mills.

The pulp and paper industry is notoriously cyclical. Hot markets are usually followed by deep freezes. In October 1993, for example, prices for Northern Bleached Softwood Kraft pulp (NBSK) bottomed out at $400 US per tonne. Prices then began a steady climb. By January 1994, prices rose to $440 US. By the end of 1994 they stood at $700 US. By October of the following year, they peaked at $985 US. Less than a year-and-a-half later, the price was back down to $565 US. And so it goes. Up and down. Up and down.

While the industry undoubtedly suffers losses when pulp markets are weak, it more than makes up for it when prices rise. It is in anticipation of high prices and high returns that companies have historically made investments to expand pulp and paper capacity. One of the more significant expansions in the coastal pulp industry occurred in the late 1980s when Canadian Forest Products joined with Japanese paper interests to build the new Howe Sound Pulp and Paper mill, to the north of Vancouver. At the time of this expansion, the forest industry across British Columbia was consuming a record number of trees. But that rate of logging has never again been repeated. Today's lower rate of cut, combined with expansions in pulp production in the Interior of the province, translates into a significant squeeze on coastal pulp producers. Simply put, the fibre pie is shrinking. There isn't enough to go around.

"The coastal industry is scraping the barrel," George Nagel, industry analyst and long-time consultant, said. "Things really started to get tight with the expansion of Howe Sound Pulp and Paper. The province-wide log harvest was running at 80 to 90 million cubic metres on public and private forestlands back then. Now it's down to perhaps 75 million cubic metres. The expansions in pulp and paper capacity in the Interior tightened up the Interior supply of chips, a portion of which had historically made its way to the coast. And that tightened things up on the coast."

The scramble for fibre was perhaps most evident during the build-up to the heady prices of 1995. At that time, pulp producers were going to extraordinary lengths to find new sources of fibre. Long-term contracts were inked with pulp-log and chip suppliers from Alaska. Loads of pulp logs from the Yukon and Northwest Territories made their way into the province. Log deliveries from Alberta and Saskatchewan were common, and log imports from as far east as Manitoba were not unheard of. This influx of out-of-province wood highlighted what has become a chronic problem for the industry and, by extension, the coastal forest. There are not enough old-growth trees to meet the forest industry's current and future needs. To keep existing mills running, all accessible old-growth forest on the coast must be cut, and then more trees from somewhere else must be found to make up the shortfall.

"The province in general faces a situation where current capacity exceeds harvest levels," a senior official of a sawmill owned by Skeena Cellulose, the company which operates a pulp mill in the northern coastal community of Prince Rupert, told the provincial government during the last great pulp boom. "This is especially true in the Prince Rupert Forest Region, where there is a documented shortfall from existing facilities of over 1 million m³ [cubic metres] per year."[5]

The other thing that occurred during the last pulp boom was that logs which could have been used to generate jobs in the sawmilling and value-added sector ended up being chipped. As Phil Musgrave, a long-time pulp buyer for Crown Zellerbach and now a pulp industry consultant

explains: "Nineteen ninety-five probably gives you a very, very good example. Pulp [logs] got up to $110 a metre. At that point, the sawmills said you can have those small logs at $110. That's more than we can pay for them. In fact, sawmills that had smaller logs in inventory sold them back into the pulp industry because lumber was off and they could not [process them] economically. It made more sense to sell them to the pulp industry."

A bust inevitably followed the heady prices of 1995. But, as the events of 1995 attest, the industry is pushing at the limits of supply. If there wasn't enough made-in-British-Columbia-fibre to go around then, there is even less today. Musgrave notes that some pulp mills in coastal B.C. have recently shipped chips from the eastern seaboard of the United States through the Panama Canal and back up the west coast to Vancouver Island. Not far to the south of the Canada-U.S. border in Bellingham, Washington, the Georgia Pacific pulp mill has shipped radiata pine chips north from as far south as Chile.

The result of this squeeze on the resource by the pulp companies is a noticeable decline in tree diameters and the age at which new or "second-growth" forests and plantations are logged, the implication of which is not lost on the Dugglebys

If all the old growth forests in B.C. were harvested, there still would be insufficient quantity to supply the pulp and paper mills in the province.
DOUG HOPWOOD

of this world. Logs from naturally re-seeded second-growth forests or plantations are smaller in diameter, with less mature wood per tree than their older counterparts. This translates into less quality wood for the production of high-value solid wood products, be it higher-value dimensional lumber or things like guitar blanks, furniture components, or doors.

One persistent question is which sector of the forest industry will command the lion's share of the fibre coming out of those new, younger forests. The speculation in some circles is that the highly-capitalized pulp industry may take the greatest share of the fibre, particularly in hot pulp markets as Musgrave points out has historically been the case. The pulp and paper sector consumes a lot of wood fibre. In 1996, it is estimated that the 24 pulp mills in the province processed the equivalent of 36.7 million cubic metres of wood (one cubic metre is equivalent in size to the average telephone pole). That translates into more than half (51.7 per cent) of all the wood coming off of publicly owned forestlands that year.[6] Such levels of consumption do not, however, translate into a lot of jobs. Province-wide, direct employment in the forest industry stood at 91,400 jobs in 1998. Only 11,000 of those positions were in the pulp and paper sector. Yet that sector consumed nearly half of all wood from the trees logged that year.[7]

The evolution of the forest industry in British Columbia and elsewhere suggests that as older and bigger trees are logged, there is increasing pressure to log the next generation of trees on shorter and shorter rotations (a rotation being the time between when a tree is planted and is logged). As rotation ages drop, so does the average diameter of the harvested logs. There may be lots of new trees out there. The industry here and elsewhere states routinely that two or more trees are planted for

The industry here and elsewhere states routinely that two or more trees are planted for every one old tree that is cut down...But that volume does not necessarily translate into lots of jobs

every one old tree that is cut down. Those new trees may represent lots of "harvestable" timber volume. But that volume does not necessarily translate into lots of jobs. It is not possible, for example, to recover from a smaller, younger log the diversity of solid wood products that can be extracted from a bigger, older log with more knot-free mature wood. If we continue our current approach to "timber management" – an approach rooted in clearcutting *all* accessible old-growth forests and converting them to rapid-growing tree farms – we may inherit a future where an increasing percentage of the total volume of wood logged goes directly to the pulp mills or to highly efficient commodity lumber mills, which process the logs before trucking or barging the chips to the pulp mills.

Furthermore, the labour required to cut down such forests is often less than is the case when older trees are logged. This is particularly true in accessible, relatively flat areas. In such settings, feller buncher machines can be employed to log second-growth coastal forests. Feller bunchers have been a fixture in the Interior for many years. But they are beginning to make their appearance on the coast, in areas of second-growth forest. One company logging a lot of coastal second-growth forest is TimberWest. Don McMullen, the company's vice-president and chief forester, said that TimberWest logs one million cubic metres of second growth a year on its Tree Farm Licence and adjacent private forest lands on Vancouver Island. Up to 70 per cent of that wood is logged using automated feller buncher machines which allow a single operator to cut down and delimb far more trees than would be logged using traditional hand-falling methods. Furthermore, some of the second-growth trees being logged are only 40 years of age and as small as 30 centimetres (11.5 inches) in diameter.[8] Duggleby said such forests are being cut far short of their potential. Some of the best fibre would be added to coastal second-growth trees at between 80 and 150 years of age. But in the rush to get the maximum volume out, the larger forest companies are logging trees on the shortest possible rotations,

then running them through commodity lumber mills and pulp mills. And they are doing so against a backdrop in which southern U.S. jurisdictions are capable of turning out trees for pulp in 12 or fewer years and lumber at around age 20.

The race to get the wood out has many coastal and Interior residents questioning the emphasis on volume over value. They're also questioning who benefits and who loses when the majority of the forest is controlled by a handful of corporations. Increasingly, those questions are fuelling demands for change in the allocation of forests and how those forests are managed. One thing prompting many communities in the region to press for change is findings published in Ministry of Forests' reports of future timber supplies. In the northwest region, there are nine Timber Supply Areas (TSAs). Each TSA is a large geographical area administered by the ministry. In most cases, it forms the operating area for a number of forest companies, each of which is entitled to log a certain volume of timber annually. If ministry analyses for each of these TSAs are an indication, the volume of available timber is falling.

Each TSA contains a graph showing the current rate of logging versus the projected "long-term" or "sustainable" rate several years or decades hence. In each case, the long-term harvest level is below the current rate, in some cases well below

(see map 3.4). When all of the current harvesting information is added together the collective logging rate in the nine TSAs is 7.99 million cubic metres. The projected long-term harvest level is 28 per cent lower, or 5.69 million cubic metres.[9]

So, less wood.

Compounding fears about a diminished wood supply is the related issue of wood quality. As TimberWest's experience suggests, the wood some communities are working with comes from younger, smaller trees. The Ministry of Forests has attempted to dampen public fears by suggesting that the timber from young forests or plantations is growing faster than expected and that the "falldown" in future logging rates noted above may not occur.[10] But falldown or no falldown, the kind of wood that coastal communities are increasingly confronted with is far different from what it once was.

So, less quality wood. And, if current patterns of resource extraction and shipment are maintained, less opportunity to work with that wood at the local level.

The northwest coast is a vast and diverse place, characterised by thousands of kilometres of mountainous coastline with long, deep inlets; and by drier mountainous and plateau settings further inland. Some parts of it, including major portions of the Haida Gwaii archipelago, the Skeena, Nass

Harvested wood from industrial logging comes from increasingly younger and smaller trees. Left: Queen Charlotte Islands logging, 1944. B.C. ARCHIVES, # F-05864 Right: Fred Linde, owner of a small modern value-added saw mill, with newly harvested trees. GARY FIEGEHEN

Barges loaded with mid-coast logs are frequently sent to mills on the southern coast, reducing the jobs available to local residents where timber is harvested.
GARY FIEGEHEN

cubic metres of annual logging activity, went to Haida Gwaii residents. In fact, only one out of four direct jobs generated from this logging activity went to local residents.[11]

The situation along the Yellowhead Highway corridor between the communities of Prince Rupert in the west and Smithers in the east is different. Here, there is an established sawmilling and pulping sector. Too much of one, some say. As noted earlier, there is a documented shortfall between what the major timber-processing facilities in the region consume each year and what is available to log on public forest lands. In fact, the shortfall approaches one million cubic metres of wood annually. The result of this so-called "overcapacity" has been the closure of medium-size and smaller mills that once employed local residents. And there is emerging consensus that further closures lie ahead (see maps 3.2 and 3.3).

Circumstances on the mid-coast are different again. Here, communities such as Bella Bella and Klemtu have witnessed little by way of extensive industrial logging. Now, having logged most of the accessible coastal forests to the south, the logging companies have arrived. The companies have offered to train people and provide jobs to local residents as loggers and road-builders, and some young people have taken advantage of the opportunity. Prospects for expanded jobs in local forest industry-related enterprises are, however, extremely limited. The limitations relate to the fact that the major forest tenure holders in the region – International Forest Products Ltd. and Western Forest Products Ltd. (Doman) – do not intend to open log-processing facilities on the mid-coast. Both companies already have established mills on Vancouver Island and Greater Vancouver that are short of timber. The intention is to log as much timber as possible on the mid-coast, and ship the raw logs south for processing. It's a situation not unlike Haida Gwaii where local residents are increasingly restless about the over-logging of their forests, logging-related losses of salmon-spawning habitat, and decreased opportunities for on-island wood-processing jobs.

and Bulkley valleys, have been extensively clearcut. Other parts, including the Kitlope watershed and the Ingram-Mooto-Ellerslie Lakes region on the mid-coast are undeveloped or only slightly altered (see map 3.1).

In the areas where major development has taken place there are, however, some significant differences. On Haida Gwaii, for example, the local wood manufacturing sector is relatively small, but has the potential to employ lots of local residents. The sector consistently faces difficulty obtaining timber, as almost all of the timber logged annually on the islands is barged to off-island interests with milling facilities on distant Vancouver Island or Greater Vancouver. Recent analysis of log flows off of Haida Gwaii suggests that more than 95 per cent of all the trees logged on the islands go to off-island interests. As a result, very few of the direct jobs associated with what, until recently, amounted to more than 2 million

Differences aside, individual communities within the three regions share something in common. They have, to varying degree, been abandoned. In Haida Gwaii the sense of abandonment is fuelled by a growing awareness of the expanse of old-growth forest already logged, and by the yearly shipment of hundreds of thousands of logs to off-island mills. On the mid-coast, abandonment is defined in the rusting hulks of long-closed canneries, such as Namu. Or the abandoned company town of Ocean Falls, where the mid-coast's only pulp mill closed two decades ago. On the Yellowhead Highway, in the Hazelton area, residents only have to drive by the Carnaby sawmill to be reminded of how forest companies so often abandon them. When Carnaby opened in the 1980s, two local sawmills and 200-plus employees lost their jobs at older mills, abandoned by the very employer who had opened the newer mill. More than a decade after its opening, Carnaby itself is in trouble. Many

local residents believe it won't be long before the mill's current owner walks away.

Confronted by depleted forests and corporate and government indifference to community stability, many residents in the northwest coast region are forging new plans and new alliances. And they are championing new proposals that they say offer a greater hope for healthy forests, and healthier more diversified local economies. The initiatives have led to some breakthroughs. The B.C. government, for example, announced the awarding of four new community forest tenures. When it said a few years ago that it would entertain letters of interest for the new tenures, the response was overwhelming. No fewer than 88 communities applied.[12] Other communities hope that legal decisions on aboriginal title and interests, combined with the lack of treaties between the Governments of Canada and B.C. and First Nations, provide a unique opportunity to forge new

Ocean Falls pulp mill, 1920s. In recent decades pulp mills throughout B.C. have been closing, leaving former employees out of work.
B.C. ARCHIVES, # G-06558

OCEAN FALLS B.C.

government-to-government relations which define a different way of doing business in the woods. Only time, community initiative, strength and capacity will determine whether the tenures of tomorrow are industrial in all but name, or something different which captures a sense of local priorities and values. But while the future is uncertain, there is no denying the present groundswell for change. More and more people say they want something better for the forest and their communities. And getting there, they believe, begins with understanding what the forest contains before you make a decision to clearcut it out of existence.

> **Only time, community initiative, strength and capacity will determine whether the tenures of tomorrow are industrial in all but name, or something different which captures a sense of local priorities and values**

If knowledge is power, Darlene Vegh, Russell Collier and Art Loring have it in spades. Vegh and Collier were until recently mapping technicians with the Strategic Watershed Analysis Team (SWAT). They worked primarily for the Gitxsan hereditary chiefs, who have been engaged in a historic legal battle with the Province of B.C. over their unsurrendered lands. Loring is intimately involved in mapping and other work in support of the Lax Skiik or Eagle clan hereditary chiefs.

During a warm, May afternoon in the mapping offices in Old Hazelton near the banks of the Skeena River, Vegh, Collier and Loring pull out map after map showing the different things they have unearthed in their study of a 25,000-hectare area, comprising the house territory of one Eagle chief. The Gitxsan call this area Luu Mii Xsugwin Gaat, which roughly translates as "the creek sides are so steep that you need a walking stick to walk along the edge." It is bordered on the east by the Skeena River, on the west by the Nass Range, on the south by the height of land separating Fiddler and Carpenter Creeks, and on the north by the height of land separating Lorne and Fiddler Creeks.

At one time, the confluence of Fiddler Creek and the Skeena River was the site of a Gitxsan village known as Gitangaat. The village was occupied for a few thousand years but is no longer there. Nearby, however, there are signs of more modern human habitation in the form of Dorreen, an old railroad and mining village. Dorreen's buildings still stand, and are occupied primarily in summer by retirees and other summer vacationers. On the periphery of the old village site, Loring said, Gitxsan people "routinely find trees that were blazed over and over again to mark ancient trails. We're still finding trees that show 400 or more years of continuous blazing." Loring has asked his chiefs for permission to construct a longhouse at the old village site. He hopes a newly built traditional structure will serve to "reactivate the waterfront" and become a "cultural tourism destination point" for people who travel to it by Indian war canoes from points up river.

Loring and others are not averse necessarily to seeing portions of Luu Mii Xsugwin Gaat logged. But they are opposed to the manner in which the Ministry of Forests and forest companies have proposed logging this and other areas in Gitxsan territory. When logging plans fail to reflect an understanding of what the forest contains, they are bad plans. Learn what is there, Loring and other Gitxsan people say. Then, and only then, decide what can be taken and how it can be taken without jeopardizing everything else.

Loring speaks from experience. For 19 years he worked in the forest industry, a dozen of them as a faller, clearcutting road-right-of-ways through the Cranberry and Nass Valleys and near the Kitlope watershed, the largest unlogged tract of temperate rainforest on B.C.'s coast. During that time he learned that "forest management" meant little more than "get the timber out." Whatever else the forest contained – salmon-spawning habitat, berries, mushrooms, culturally-modified trees, and on and on – was subservient to that one interest. And it was reflected in the ravages visited on the land. "After seeing all of the destruction, I made a decision. I had to change my lifestyle and work on the struggle my people were in," Loring said. Today, as land and resources advisor for Lax Skiik, he coordinates ground research and inventory work in support of clan initiatives.

Critical to that work is the mapping done by Art Loring, assisted by Vegh and Collier. For Luu Mii Xsugwin Gaat, Loring prepared numerous maps showing a range of important resources in the region. There are stretches along Fiddler Creek, for example, which are used by spawning coho salmon. The salmon species is at critically low numbers in many tributaries of the Skeena as it is elsewhere in British Columbia. The same stretches of Fiddler Creek are also home to bald eagles, and mountain goat. And this area, like other sensitive sites in the region, is precisely where the local logging company proposes building its road. "Between 35 and 40 goats are found in this section year-round," Loring said, pointing at the map and a bend in Fiddler Creek. "And this section overlaps with the salmon and eagle habitat. With the proposed logging, there's really no protection for the fish, eagles or goats."

On other maps developed for the Gitxsan, Loring identified important areas for moose, grizzly bear, fur-bearers such as marten, huckleberries, soapberries and cedar trees. "These six-to-seven-foot-diameter cedar may be between 800 and 1,000 years old," Loring said. "They are big, valuable trees. And they are also critically important trees for First Nations. We as a tribe depend very much on arts and crafts. We'll continue to need these trees for totems and other purposes. And we *don't* want to see them logged."

Having said this, the Eagleclan have used mapping and related inventory work to identify 13 distinct places within the 25,000-hetare area where logging of some kind (not necessarily clearcutting) could take place. They have even gone to the effort of identifying how much timber they feel may be sustainably logged from these areas – about 5,000 cubic metres every five years. That level of logging, Loring and others say, can occur without threatening local wildlife. Furthermore, it can be done without harming other forest resources of commercial

value such as pine mushrooms, which are regularly gathered for sale by Gitxsan people and other area residents.

As Loring returns to a long table littered with maps and mylar in the Gitxsan's mapping office, he looks down at the colourful computer-generated images before him. "As you go through each layer," he told a visitor, "you can see the significance of this area for wildlife and fish. And the presence of wildlife and fish often coincides with riparian zones at the foot of very steep slopes. These areas are not suitable for logging roads. On the other hand, on the relatively flat and stable bench lands elsewhere in the region, some logging-related development might make sense" (see map 3.5).

"What we're saying with all of this work is you can't, in every watershed, expect to take out timber," Loring continued. "But that's not what the Ministry of Forests said."

Indeed not. In fact, in this part of the world Ministry of Forests officials have scuttled Gitxsan-supported initiatives aimed at redefining how business is conducted in the region's forests. In mainstream media accounts, the Gitxsan's modern-day struggle with forest companies and the Ministry of Forests has often been framed to suggest that Gitxsan actions, including occasional high-profile blockades of logging roads, are all about stopping development. But as Gitxsan mapping initiatives attest, this is too simplistic a portrayal. In fact Gitxsan hereditary chiefs, including those of the Eagle clan, have worked to forge new relations with local industry and local non-aboriginal governments. In doing so, they have arrived at land use plans that all three groups thought made sense.

In the early 1990s, one of the region's logging and sawmilling businesses hired a professional forester by the name of Fred Philpott. Philpott's job was to come up with new logging plans for a five-year period. What Philpott submitted on behalf of Bud Hobenshield and Kitwanga Lumber Co. Ltd. represented a radical departure for logging companies in the region. Philpott's so-called Total Chance Plan (TCP) called for the company to stay out of

It was an admirable effort to accommodate a range of human interests. But it was in vain.

several areas in Eagle territory where previous logging had damaged forests and forest streams. The plan also proposed that half of all future logging be selective. In other words, individual trees would be logged amid standing trees, with the objective being to maintain the forest's structure – its diversity of tree species, ages and sizes. It called for greater protection of older forests, protection of riparian areas, and more.

In developing and selling the plan to the public, Philpott made it clear that a priority for Kitwanga Lumber was to devise plans that met with the approval of the Eagle chiefs. "We will cooperatively work with Lax Skiik to develop mutually satisfactory silvicultural systems and pre-harvest silvicultural systems," Philpott said in a letter to Lax Skiik in July 1992. "Much of this will be accomplished through our joint cooperative Total Chance Development Plans. We have no intentions to implement silvicultural systems and prescriptions that are not satisfactory to Lax Skiik and we will co-operate with Lax Skiik during all phases of the planning and cutting permit development operations."[13]

It was this approach to planning which would later result in praise from individuals inside and outside of government. Typical of those supporting the plan was Leonard Vanderstar, a forest ecosystem specialist with the former Ministry of Environment's regional offices in Smithers. "I feel that this plan will serve as a role model for our future forests," Vanderstar wrote to Philpott in March 1994. "The plan illustrates the compatibility of timber extraction with maintenance of wildlife habitat, recreational opportunities, and recognition of local culture."[14]

Two months later came this comment from Bill Fell, president of the Seven Sisters Society, a local conservation group committed to protecting the renowned and spectacular seven-peaked mountain range and surrounding forest west of Hazelton:

"The high quality forest planning by F.A.C. Philpott is the acceptable …[level of] planning for this region. We are pleased with the selective logging systems on sensitive sites. The designation of biodiversity zones and protected riparian corridors on the total chance plans is admirable."[15]

In a series of public presentations, Philpott listened to, and incorporated responses from a range of interests including Lax Skiik. He did so over almost two years, building public support and a level of trust with Lax Skiik that has yet to be replicated. It was an admirable effort to accommodate a range of human interests. Philpott had learned to live in the same body inhabited by Lax Skiik. But his efforts were in vain.

In June 1994, two years after he submitted his plans to the Ministry of Forest's Kispiox Forest District offices in Hazelton, Philpott finally received a reply. It came in the form of a letter of rebuke rejecting Kitwanga Lumber's plans. "The self-imposed [logging] restrictions have reduced the operating area of each of your charts by 20% on average. The Total Chance Plans must be revised and the amount of operable forest unnecessarily tied up in [unlogged forest] reserves and various corridors [for wildlife] reduced to the 12% figure stated in the Kispiox Resource Management Plan," George Burns, the Ministry's district operations manager said.[16]

Burns was unprepared to accept any reduction in logging rates. Nor would he entertain notions of logging half of the region's forests using alternative, non-clearcutting methods. Burns termed the proposal "far in excess" of Ministry targets "which clearly state that clearcutting and thus even aged management will continue to be the predominant silvicultural system in the Kispiox TSA."

In a letter of reply three months later, Philpott warned the Ministry that rejection of his plans would almost certainly result in a "tremendous loss of credibility for the Kitwanga Lumber Co. Ltd. with the Native Hereditary Chiefs and with the general public throughout the working area."[17] The list of special features in the region's forests to which Philpott had tried to offer a modicum of protection included: wetlands, important wintering and calving areas for larger animals such as moose, recreational and traditional trails, key movement corridors for wildlife through valley-bottom forests, areas of high visual and archaeological importance, ancient Native burial grounds and Native medicinal plants. "We believe it is better to err on the side of conservation, with the option of additional and careful development in the future, planned on the basis of fuller knowledge regarding habitat requirements and biodiversity than presently exists, than to commit ourselves to maximum development immediately, and therefore foreclose on future options."

District forests ministry officials didn't see things that way, however. Nor, apparently, did Skeena Cellulose's predecessor, Repap, which owned the nearby Carnaby sawmill and the pulp mill in distant Prince Rupert. Repap bought a controlling interest in Kitwanga Lumber, and before long Philpott found his progressive, community-supported plans shunted aside. Philpott continued to press more senior levels of the ministry to take a hard look at his plans. In an April 1995 letter to Larry Pedersen, the province's chief forester, he warned that the provincial government was being shortsighted in supporting Repap's plans. "If the total chance plan that I submitted remains NOT ACCEPTED by the Kispiox District, and is changed and degraded by Repap Carnaby Inc. to the level of their own plan, the opportunity to progress, and to have an example within this District that does work and is accepted by all groups, is lost for several more years. Conventional development plans and cutting plans, forcing clearcut harvesting as the primary silvicultural system, paying lip service to aboriginal rights, and backed up with court injunctions and lawyers is not going to solve the problem…[and] the opportunities to log without harassment and possible violence will become less and less."[18]

Included in the letter was a suggestion that the ministry consider offering forest companies incentives in the form of reduced stumpage to reflect the added costs of more detailed planning and selective logging. Philpott also said that senior ministry officials should reconsider the district's decision. But ultimately both the Chief Forester of B.C. and then Forests Minister Andrew Petter rejected his suggestions. It was back to business as usual. Back to clearcutting, and extracting big volumes of timber. Back to generating the maximum stumpage fees to government and forest companies down the road as they tried to force their way into places like Luu Mii Xsugwin Gaat.

A half-hour drive south from Hazelton lies the community of Moricetown. Above the highway beyond the houses, a dirt road rounds a curve and ends at a large clearing in the bush. At the end of the clearing stands a new industrial building clad in dark blue sheet metal. This is Kyahwood Forest Products, a joint venture between the Wet'suwet'en First Nation's Moricetown band and Prince-George-headquartered Northwood Inc. (now Canfor). This same patch of ground used to be home to a small sawmill that once employed local residents. But like so much else in these parts, the mill and its workers fell victim to the arrival of bigger and more automated commodity lumber mills. The mill closed in the early 1980s, putting many people out of work.

New approaches to forestry are emerging on the northwest coast. Kyahwood Forest Products in Moricetown is a value added mill jointly owned by First Nations and industry.
TERRY LALONDE

"We came into a community with an unemployment rate of 85 to 90 per cent. Many of the people here hadn't worked for as long as five years prior to our coming here. There was a lot of groundwork that had to be done and training levels brought up just for people to start work here," said Kyahwood's office administrator, Deb Frazer.

Donning the obligatory hard hat, Frazer takes the visitor on a tour of the new mill. Walking on overhead steel walkways, she explains the intricacies of this value-added mill's production. Kyahwood is what is known in industry circles as a finger-jointing plant. Its wood comes primarily from "trim ends" supplied by Canfor's Houston sawmill, which at an estimated annual output of 1.5 million cubic metres of lumber, is one of the bigger commodity mills in the province. Trim ends are the short or broken ends of lumber that are below acceptable length or grade for sale. Prior to the start up of the joint venture, Canfor chipped this material for conversion into pulp. In a finger-jointing mill, the trim ends are chopped to set lengths, and

then zigzag cut at each end. After this the ends are glued and pressed together to make full length boards. Each glued wood piece fits tightly into the next, much like your fingers do when you slide one hand's set between the other's.

Walking outside and inside the Kyahwood mill it is hard not to get swept up in the physical accomplishment and energy of the venture. A new building heated with a high-temperature, wood-fired furnace keeps the mill at a constant 65 degrees Fahrenheit – a must if the newly fingered joints are to set properly. An enthusiastic workforce of 60 men and women, almost all of them Wet'suwet'en people, most of them young, anchors the new venture. Majority control of the business rests in local hands. And all of this rises out of the ashes of a defunct mill in a community with a history of chronic unemployment and poor prospects for new jobs.

"There seems to be an incredible pride of ownership," Frazer said, leaning in close to shout over whining saws and the clang of trim ends falling into big metal sort bins. "People are happy

At work at Kyahwood Forest Products.
LEN FRAZER

to be working. Up to Christmas, we had an absenteeism rate nobody could beat. Nobody was off work at all."

Back at her office, Frazer offers more details on the $6.7-million joint venture. A management committee made up of two representatives each from Northwood and the Moricetown band applied for and received nearly $500,000 in Forest Renewal BC funds to train prospective employees. The money from the Crown corporation allowed people to gain requisite training in lumber grading and other aspects of value-added lumber production as well as industrial first aid training and certification. The money also covered about 75 per cent of the wages during the mill's initial start up.

Today, Kyahwood's workers earn between $10.66 and $20.71 an hour. And, because the facility is located on-reserve, no payroll taxes are deducted. The mill was built in 1996, with full production commencing in January 1997. There are currently 60 hourly employees and six management staff at the facility. A very small amount of the mill's output is headed for Japan. But the majority is destined for Chicago and points east. Much of the mill's production – the finger-jointed two-by threes, two-by-fours and two-by-fives – will end up in residential construction projects, some in the pre-fab walls of mobile homes. If all goes to plan and Kyahwood meets its projected annual production of 414,000 m³, 85 hourly workers will be employed at the facility. Looking at the zeal with which the mill's workers apply themselves, it is easy to envision the mill meeting or exceeding the target, and as many as 25 more people finding work in Moricetown and area.

As beneficial as the joint-venture is to Moricetown's residents, it is equally if not more so to Canfor. The benefits to Canfor come in at least two forms. The first and most obvious is that a new product is manufactured which Canfor can sell at a considerable profit during peaks in the North American residential construction market. (To boot, it's being created by a workforce trained at little if any cost to the company, thanks to dollars

from Forest Renewal.) Less obvious but equally important is that Canfor is the principal beneficiary of a new allotment of timber through the ministry's small business program (described above). On paper, the recipient of this timber sale is the joint-venture running Kyahwood. The joint-venture received 80,000 cubic metres of wood over a three-year period which ended at the end of 1998. A second licence awarded under the same program granted the joint-venture a further 160,000 cubic metres of wood over an eight-year period. All of that wood is scheduled to be processed in Canfor's facilities, and in return for that wood, Canfor will provide sufficient trim ends to Kyahwood to run its operation. So far from these two "small business" sales, Canfor has received an additional 240,000 cubic metres of logs to run through its sawmills and sell to its customers. All it was obligated to do in return, was provide trim ends to Kyahwood. If Kyahwood wasn't there, the trim ends could just as easily have been sold to another operation producing a similar product. Or they could have been chipped and turned into pulp.

As tangible as the benefits of this joint-venture are to the Moricetown band and Canfor, there is something oddly disquieting at Kyahwood. And it relates to the one ingredient that must be there in order to keep the whole operation afloat, namely, wood. Without it, the mill can't survive. This raises questions about how the forests are managed to provide the wood that feeds the mill. And beyond that, who ultimately makes those management decisions.

Don Ryan, chief negotiator for the Gitxsan First Nation, said that those decisions must include the Gitxsan and Wet'suwet'en hereditary chiefs whose house territories are or will be impacted by industrial logging activity. And the decisions must pertain to *all* of those lands. Ryan said he and other

An enthusiastic workforce of 60 men and women, almost all of them Wet'suwet'en people, most of them young, anchors the new venture

Mid-coast logs float down the lower Fraser River to be processed at mills in southern B.C.
GARY FIEGEHEN

our territory are the result of human intervention, our people doing controlled burns over the years. You can see what people have been doing for 200, 300, 400, years, just by looking at the trees on the landscape. You can see the blazes on trees that go back 400 years. You can see trails, roadways, trading routes, village sites, water supply sites, that go back centuries. And you can see where people were rotating their communities. They would stay in one place for a thousand years and then move on. They were trying to fit into the landscape. And the house territories played a very dominant role in that. They need to play a dominant role again."

If you look at the recent history of the forest industry in the Moricetown and Hazelton regions, it is not encouraging, Ryan continues. Perhaps the most telling example of the government and forest industry overstepping the bounds of sound management was the approval and construction of the Carnaby sawmill, a short distance west of Hazelton. In 1987, when Westar Timber Ltd. opened the new state-of-the-art commodity lumber mill, the Ministry of Forests issued a press release in which it told local residents that the new mill would "eliminate the uncertainty in this remote community and stabilize employment."[19]

Just the opposite happened. Less than one year after Carnaby opened, 100 mill workers at Westar's nearby Rim sawmill lost their jobs. Shortly after that, an equal number of workers at the Kitwanga sawmill were off the job. The layoffs came as no surprise to people like Ryan who knew there wasn't the timber to supply Carnaby, let alone the other two mills. Prior to Carnaby opening, Westar had conducted its own timber supply analysis, which showed that the region's forests could only supply a fraction of the wood needed to keep Carnaby afloat. In fact, the projected shortfall was in the neighbourhood of 4,400 truck loads of logs per year.[20] The only way the company could keep Carnaby going was to close the other two sawmills and then try to convince the Ministry of Forests to redirect wood that was headed to sawmills in Prince George to the Hazelton area instead. Westar lost

Gitxsan and Wet'suwet'en leaders are not interested in participating in a modern-day treaty negotiation process which sees First Nations given cash and exclusive ownership of a fraction of their traditional territories. "We're interested in co-management with British Columbia and Canada. And we're interested in revenue sharing. But we're not into a land selection model. They have to be prepared to accept the model that we have put forward for the management of our territory. The model is based on our house groups and house territories. And it's co-management of those territories that we're after and want to complete through a negotiation process with the Governments of Canada and British Columbia."

"Co-management means understanding the concerns of our people," Ryan continued, "particularly the house groups. Because it's their land that we're taking the trees from. We have to look after those territories. The Gitxsan and Wet'suwet'en nations have been managing the land for thousands of years. They have left their mark. A lot of the trees on the ground in

"The Gitxsan and Wet'suwet'en nations have been managing the land for thousands of years"

that bid, and ultimately sold Carnaby to Repap, Skeena Cellulose's predecessor.

Ryan, Loring and others in the Hazelton area are troubled by what has happened at Carnaby and Skeena Cellulose. They are convinced that there is a better way of doing things. And it begins with changing the way forest tenures are allocated in order that communities themselves have a significant say in what happens to the forests surrounding them. Without that say, joint ventures such as Kyahwood are subject to the whim of government and corporate interests, and, Kyahwood runs the risk of going the route of the Rim sawmill and mills elsewhere that closed when the trees grew scarce and corporate tenure holders "consolidated" operations.

In the Hazelton region, in Haida Gwaii, in Prince Rupert and elsewhere, long-time residents have lived to see the wholesale logging of much of their old-growth forests. They've lived to learn that old-growth forests and all the rich arboreal, terrestrial and marine life they shelter are in danger of being eliminated from much or all of their historic range. Elsewhere, the history of industrial logging activity dates back only a few years, not decades. People in the communities of Bella Bella and Klemtu have long seen barges heading south laden with logs from more northern climes such as Haida Gwaii and Prince Rupert. Now they're watching an increasing number of barges carrying logs from their back yard head down the coast to southern mills. And they are being bombarded with out-of-region visitors telling them what they should or shouldn't do.

Some of these visitors are representatives of the major forest companies that propose to log the region's forests, many of which are in coastal valleys that have yet to see roads or clearcuts. These visitors have weighed in with proposals to train members of local First Nations for work as road-builders and loggers. Some of their proposals have met with

initial approval of elected bodies such as the Heiltsuk Tribal Council. In a move similar to that in Moricetown, the band and Western Forest Products (WFP) joined together to obtain Forest Renewal funds to train prospective employees. As a result of that funding, there were 15 Heiltsuk people in Bella Bella who were working on WFP logging crews on Yeo Island in the Spring of 1998. Another two Heiltsuk people obtained jobs helping WFP build a road into the Ingram-Mooto, one of the largest unlogged stretches of temperate rainforest on the mid-coast. "They are paid according to union scale," Arlene Wilson, the Heiltsuk Tribal Council's former chief councillor said of the local men who picked up work in the logging industry. "It's been a boom to us, because of the economic spin-offs that have come back to us."

Other visitors have arrived with a much different message. Various conservation groups have urged band council leaders, Heiltsuk hereditary chiefs and others to stop WFP and other logging companies from going into the region's untouched forested valleys. They have carried that message not only to local residents, but also to the international arena where they have attempted to get European, American and Japanese consumers of forest products produced by WFP and other companies to halt their purchases. Some of them have also mounted road blockades to try to prevent or slow forest companies from logging areas of the mid-coast forest to the south of Bella Bella.

The blockades have had a galvanizing effect in communities such as Bella Bella. On the one hand, there is resentment at the perceived arrogance of outsiders coming in and saying that what Western and their Heiltsuk partners did is wrong. That they should stop and forgo the new, high-paying local logging jobs. "They tell me that they're not supposed to be logging. But they haven't given us alternatives," Wilson said at the time. "Everybody has their own game to play. But it's not our game. Jurisdiction and co-management of local resources. That's what we're after, so we have a stronger say in how our lands are managed."

On the other hand, the blockades and overseas consumer campaigns appear to have reinforced what other leaders in Bella Bella, including a number of hereditary chiefs, have long felt. That is, that industrial logging is proceeding too rapidly, and without proper input from Heiltsuk people, who have intimate knowledge of what lies in their territory, and have been putting that information into their own maps and documents.

Such feelings began to be expressed more forcefully in February 1997 when seven hereditary chiefs of the Heiltsuk Nation wrote Haindl Papier, a major German paper producer, saying: "It has come to our attention that your company is a major buy [er] of the wood products from Western Forest Products. We would like to inform you that we oppose clearcut logging in our traditional territory. We are still negotiating a treaty and are asking that a one-year moratorium be established in order for our community to work together for a short and long term development plan for our forest and sea resources."[21]

In another letter in February 1998, the hereditary chiefs commended Wilson for her dedicated work on behalf of Heiltsuk people. But they also said that it was imperative more work be done to determine whether or not WFP should be logging in Heiltsuk traditional territory, and if so, where and under what conditions. "It has come to our attention that there are long-term plans to clearcut log this central coast area and this will have a great impact on the sustainability of a future foundation for our generations to come. While we support logging in a sustainable way, we feel that this decision has such long-standing effects that the whole community should be informed of the plans and should be involved in making the decisions about entering into any partnerships to clearcut log. Not only does logging affect the land, it has negative effect on the water and its resources as streams and creeks get clogged or log dump sites disturb nature's life cycle."[22]

The letter urged that a referendum be conducted to poll Heiltsuk people about whether or not the First Nation's traditional territory should be clearcut; that a one-year moratorium on further clearcutting be imposed during which time the Heiltsuk could come up with their own alternate logging plans; that alternate employment opportunities be explored; and that the Heiltsuk people be fully informed of the short- and long-term impacts of logging their traditional territory.

Not long after that letter went into the mail, representatives with various conservation groups began an ultimately successful campaign to convince the region's major logging companies to accept a temporary halt to logging. In the summer of 2000, the companies, with the then notable exception of International Forest Products, agreed to a moratorium during which time negotiations would be held between the companies and conservationists to come up with a new plan for forestry in the mid-coast region.

To highlight the concerns of the hereditary chiefs, more than 60 people including Heiltsuk hereditary chiefs staged a demonstration in April 1998, on the new road being built into the Ingram-Mooto by WFP. The demonstration, in which some chiefs participated, received no publicity. But it was a powerful demonstration nonetheless. It temporarily stopped WFP from proceeding, and it forced the company to confront the fact that, despite the logging jobs then held by some Heiltsuk people, there was still considerable concern within Heiltsuk territory about the company's plans. No member of Greenpeace or any other outside environmental group participated in the event. It was a statement made by and for the Heiltsuk people.

Like any community confronted with sudden change, there are and will continue to be differences over how to proceed. But within the Heiltsuk Nation there appears to be at least one common point of understanding. As Wilson said, the Heiltsuk people want a substantial say in what

"Not only does logging affect the land, it has negative effect on the water and its resources as streams and creeks get clogged or log dump sites disturb nature's life cycle"

As fewer trees are available along the northern coast, unsustainable logging practices are now moving into the central coast of B.C. Yeo Island, Heiltsuk Traditional Territory.
DAVE NUNUK

happens in their territory. And they want it now, while they still have options. "We continue to maintain that we must be a part of the management structure and have a say in what goes on in our territory," Wilson said.

In the opinion of Heiltsuk hereditary chiefs, having a meaningful say begins with knowledge. You must know what is there. And you must know what the implications of various management methods are. How will those methods affect what is on the land and in the water? How will they impact on the existing social and business structure in place in Heiltsuk territory? For instance, will operation of Bella Bella's expanding fish-processing plant be jeopardised by clearcut logging activity that has proven time-and-time-again to damage spawning beds in rivers and streams? These questions are not easily answered. Which is why the chiefs have asked for time during which information can be properly gathered and discussed.

Time may indeed now be on the chiefs' side. In April 2001, the B.C. government announced a sweeping land-use plan for the mid-coast which, in addition to ruling out logging activity in various areas, placed a moratorium on logging elsewhere pending the development of "ecosystem-based" forestry plans.

The government also signed a protocol with six First Nations whose members live in an area ranging from Cape Caution in the south to the Alaska border in the north, including Haida Gwaii. Said then Premier Ujjal Dosanjh: "This Protocol Agreement will establish a leadership role for First Nations in remaining land-use decisions and ongoing management, helping ensure that future decisions respect the region's

Haida Gwaii loggers have definitively proven that it is possible to selectively log old-growth forests while leaving behind lots of trees to protect forest-dependent wildlife and important fish-bearing streams

Pine mushrooms are one example of non-timber forest products – ways in which forests can generate income beyond logging alone.
SIGNY FREDRICKSON

unique environmental, cultural, tourism and recreation values."

If Dosanjh's words are more than just government spin, if coastal First Nations do end up playing a more substantive role in determining the nature of resource industry activities in this remote wild land, substantive change may be in order.

There are, of course, alternatives to the industrial cut-and-run model promoted by WFP and others.

Contrary to the assertions of the major forest companies and their public relations experts, big trees in old-growth forests can be selectively logged. On some of the most wind-exposed, steep and unstable slopes in Haida Gwaii loggers have definitively proven that it is possible to selectively log old-growth forests while leaving

Oona River's community forest proposal is meant to address concerns at the local level where they most properly belong

behind lots of trees to protect forest-dependent wildlife and important fish-bearing streams. And to make money while doing it. The provincial government is more than aware of this. It has monitored selective logging trials elsewhere in the province, including the Hazelton area near where Fred Philpott devised his forward-thinking forestry plans. One hitch against this approach to forestry is that it costs more to plan and implement. But the government, which sets the stumpage fees that logging companies pay for the trees they cut on public lands, can lower the fees to reflect higher costs.

North of Bella Bella, people like Terry Garon have come to understand that the forest has the potential to generate lots of income without being clearcut. Garon's vision is to manage a woodlot up the Skeena River from Prince Rupert. He wants to selectively log it, and not for the timber so much as for the valuable, much-in-demand mushrooms he plans to cultivate. From the back of his remodelled kitchen in his neat Victorian home, Garon takes the visitor to a backyard shack. Inside the darkened interior, shelves are lined with black plastic bags punctured with holes out of which grow shitake and oyster mushrooms. The mushrooms sell for between $20 and $40 a kilogram. Garon wants to log and buck alder trees in his woodlot, then drill the alder and plug it with spores that will sprout crops of mushrooms. He knows of other medicinal plants and native mushrooms in the forest that he hopes to market as well. It's a far cry from the work Garon once did on a helicopter logging crew, pulling 3,500 tonnes of top quality Sitka spruce out of one coastal valley in a single eight-hour shift. Garon said he was astonished by a visit he made to Merv Wilkinson's woodlot on east Vancouver Island. The woodlot has gained world renown for the manner in which it has been selectively logged. "That place is *amazing*," Garon said. "The woodlot has been selectively logged for several decades and it maintains the structure of an older forest with a diversity of tree species of different ages."

South and east of Prince Rupert in the community of Oona River on Porcher Island, local residents have banded together to propose a community forest on the island. Residents such as Jan Lemon were at the forefront of that campaign, as well as another successful on-island initiative to restore the island's once-strong salmon runs. Now in its 18th year of operation, the Oona River hatchery has helped boost local coho salmon stocks. In the spring of 1998, there were 12,000 coho fry in two tanks at the hatchery bordering the river. Those fry, along with another 28,000 fry at a second hatchery at Kumealon Inlet, were scheduled to be released into the wild later that season.

Staring down at the fish milling in the cool waters of their stainless steel tanks, Lemon talks about the success of the hatchery program. "The first year, returns doubled. And the next generation, they tripled," Lemon said with pride. "We're not sure why Oona River has fish coming back as good as it does. But we've been enhancing an October-spawning coho run and they're not getting intercepted by the commercial fleet." Lemon goes on to say that the demise of Oona River's salmon relates to too many commercial fishing openings in the wrong places at the wrong times. Now that the salmon are coming back, bird populations are on an upswing. There are more eagles, more herons, more mergansers. But now that the hatchery is helping bring local fish and wildlife stocks back, Lemon is casting her mind to the potential threat of habitat destruction should unchecked logging destroy local spawning beds. Oona River's community forest proposal is meant to address those concerns at the local level where they most properly belong. At the time Oona River submitted its proposal, the Ministry of Forests had yet to announce its community forest tenure initiative. Consequently, it offered a woodlot to a local family who runs a small mill on the island. The licence will give the mill 1,000 cubic metres of wood per year, which represents a start toward self-sufficiency for two resident families. The woodlot is not free of controversy because it crosses several salmon streams, Lemon said. But it's a step in the right direction in that it gives tenure to local residents. A community woodlot would only increase the benefits by turning over a wider area of forest to be managed for the multitude of benefits local residents derive from a healthy, well-cared-for forest.

It seems that when the government wants to it can assert that the forests of the province do, indeed, belong to the people

East of Rupert along the Yellowhead Highway corridor, a report points to the value of value-added. It is, as the oft-repeated credo says, possible to do more with less. The 1997 report prepared for Forest Renewal BC notes that 11 value-added facilities were running or contemplated opening on the highway corridor between Prince Rupert and Francois Lake to the south of Burns Lake. Those facilities were projected to employ 327 people.[23] The facilities made a range of products from high-end laminated pine toys, boxes and cabinets, to joinery and pine furniture stock, to finger-jointed boards, to panelling and strip flooring. The combined output of these facilities was in the neighbourhood of 780,000 cubic metres annually, meaning one direct job for every 2,400 cubic metres of production. By comparison, just one commodity sawmill in the same study area required 4,800 cubic metres of production to sustain one job.[24] While joint-ventures in logging employ people, they don't come close to generating the jobs that are created when logs are broken down into finished products, particularly high-end items.

More wood can be allocated to the ministry's small business program to make more of these value-added ventures a reality. This would almost certainly involve taking additional wood away from the tenure holders, as was done more than a decade ago when the program was expanded. Or the provincial government might embark on a different course by changing existing forest tenures in ways that encourage the major companies to make more higher value products themselves or in new joint ventures along the lines of Kyahwood.

Whatever option is chosen, it will almost certainly require careful monitoring to ensure that new jobs are, indeed being created. And it will require strong political leadership. When the last so-called "takeback" of wood occurred, the big forest companies cried foul. They claimed contracts had been broken and that investor confidence in the industry would be shattered. There was enormous pressure on the government to scuttle the initiative. But it held firm. And in time just the opposite of what the industry predicted happened. The industry managed record profits over the next years. And, despite cries of broken contracts, no compensation was offered or paid by the B.C. government. It seems that when the government wants to it can assert that the forests of the province do, indeed, belong to the people. And furthermore, that they can and should be managed for public

> **While joint-ventures in logging employ people, they don't come close to generating the jobs that are created when logs are broken down into finished products, particularly high-end items**

benefit. During the provincial administration of Mike Harcourt, a multi-party legislative committee recommended taking more wood away from the major tenure holders and turning it over to the small business program to fuel more value-added initiatives. But this time the government bowed to pressure from unionized woodworking and corporate interests. It quashed the plan.

Back in the North Pacific Cannery cafe, Duggelby sips his coffee and talks about the future. As I listen, I'm struck by the similarities he shares with his neighbour and friend Terry Garon. Both men roll with the challenges confronting them. They try new things. They dream new dreams. Duggelby has gone from working on the railroad, to making wooden guitar tops, to becoming a small business logger, to owning and operating a bed and breakfast lodge and adjacent cafe, to organising and outfitting kayak trips for visitors to the Prince Rupert area. He dreams of returning to guitar-top making, and possibly cutting wood for use in the manufacture of piano sound boards.

Garon has worked as a silvicultural contractor thinning trees. He's done a stint on a helicopter logging crew. He and his wife owned and operated a successful bed, bath and linen shop, which would still be running today if it hadn't been torched by an arsonist. He's got an industrial first aid ticket and works as a first-aid attendant at the nearby pulp mill. He's opened a new business with his wife, a store where they sell native and local art among other things. He runs boat tours and hikes up various tributaries of the Skeena River. He's grown mushrooms for sale. And he dreams of one day running his own selectively-logged woodlot where he can grow mushrooms in the cool, moist air of the Skeena River valley's forest.

As Duggelby sips on another coffee he talks about what lies ahead. He needs to work a season or two more in the tourism trade. He needs to raise enough money, he figures, to buy a good state-of-the-art band saw. It'll cost him $66,000. Then, if he can get those precious three to five logs a year, it's back to cutting guitar tops and keeping three families in good money.

But Duggelby doesn't stop there. There's so much more that could be done, he said. "When you look around at the profile of the forest up here, you find that about 20 per cent of the trees are H Grade or I Grade. We should be turning those trees into piano wood, right here in Prince Rupert. Right now, a company in Oregon that doesn't have any of its own wood is a major supplier to Yamaha Pianos in Georgia. They're buying logs out of Howe Sound, then running them through a so-called 'custom-cut' mill in Vancouver, which basically means that they're turning a round log into a square log. And then they go to Oregon, where the real value is extracted turning the square logs into pieces which are laminated together to make the sound boards in pianos. It's bloody ridiculous that we're not doing that here, in B.C."

A short distance away from the cannery, West Fraser Timber Co. Ltd. runs a sawmill in an industrial park on the outskirts of Prince Rupert. After visiting Duggelby, I drive by the mill to have a look at what, exactly, it is producing. I find what Duggelby told me I would. Stack upon stack of square logs; big pieces of wood that have had little more than their rounded outer layers hived off. At the dawn of the 21st century, one of the largest forest companies in the province is content to barely scratch the surface of adding value to the centuries-old trees it is cutting down by the tens of thousands each year.

Not far from the West Fraser sawmill, the Skeena Cellulose pulp mill lurches along, barely keeping ahead of its creditors. During a visit to the region, newspapers were filled with reports about a new round of layoffs at the troubled mill, and an announcement by the mill management that wood, chemical and service suppliers must cut their billings in order to keep the operation afloat. The request was made despite the fact that the suppliers collectively were out millions of dollars in payments as a result of the company filing for bankruptcy protection the year before. The forest and residents of the north coast continue to pay an enormous price to keep the mill operating. This, despite the overwhelming evidence of a growing fibre shortfall in the region. This, despite the assertion of a former chemical engineer at the mill who alleged that a new mill could produce the same amount of pulp with half the wood fibre presently consumed. The provincial government knew all this, yet decided to commit $350-million of public money to the foundering mill anyway.

To keep the pulp mill going, lots of trees will have to be cut down before their time, chipped in their adolescence instead of worked in their prime. The thought of that has the adaptive Duggelby shaking his head. "A lot of the wood on the coast that's so-called 'pulp' would be good wood in 50 years. Thirty to 50-year-old trees are cut by the millions on this coast every year. If we left them alone for 50 years, they'd be extremely valuable. It's *madness* to be cutting those trees now."

In the face of that madness Duggelby, Garon, Lemon, Loring, Ryan and many others dream new dreams. Unlike those who unquestioningly prop up the old, they try to do something new. And not just for them, but for all of us. The places they call home are special. They are the organs and appendages of a body that millions of us share, a body we've come to call British Columbia. We allow their forests to be degraded, their waters to be despoiled, their aspirations and initiatives to be scuttled, at considerable cost to them and to us. For their sake, the rest of us need to learn to inhabit a new and shared body, to understand the unique character of that body's many parts in order that it can be nurtured and sustained.

> **To keep the pulp mill going, lots of trees will have to be cut down before their time, chipped in their adolescence instead of worked in their prime**

REFERENCES

1 B.C. Ministry of Forests, 2000. Provincial Linkage AAC Report.

2 Ministry of Forests. 1996, 1997, 1998. Small Business Forest Enterprise Program disposals, North Coast Forest District.

3 Patricia Marchak as quoted in "Pulp Prospects". March 7-14, 1996. *The Georgia Straight*.

4 Major Primary Timber Processing Facilities in British Columbia, 1996. Ministry of Forests' Economics and Trade Branch, April, 1997. See also Data on the Corporate Concentration of Harvesting Rights, Manufacturing Capacity and Ownership in the B.C. Forest Industry. Forest Resources Commission Background Papers – Volume 5, March, 1991.

5 Dan Tuomi as quoted in "The Cassiar: British Columbia's Fragile and Imperiled Northern Wilderness" March, 1996. *BC Wild*.

6 Major Timber Processing Facilities in British Columbia, 1996; and Data on the Corporate Concentration of Harvesting Rights.

7 1998. *The Forest Industry in British Columbia*. Price Waterhouse Coopers, Inc.

8 Ben Parfitt. 1998. *Forest Follies: Adventures and Misadventures in the Great Canadian Forest.* Harbour Publishing.

9 From Kalum South TSA Timber Supply Analysis, Ministry of Forests, June, 1994; Morice TSA Timber Supply Analysis, Ministry of Forests, February, 1996; North Coast TSA Timber Supply Analysis, Ministry of Forests, January, 1994; Lakes TSA Timber Supply Analysis, Ministry of Forests, June, 1995; Bulkley TSA Timber Supply Analysis, Ministry of Forests, August, 1993; Cranberry Timber Supply Area Analysis Report, Ministry of Forests, November, 1997; Mid Coast Timber Supply Analysis, Ministry of Forests, May, 1993; Kispiox TSA Timber Supply Analysis, Ministry of Forests, August, 1996; Queen Charlotte TSA Timber Supply Analysis, Ministry of Forests, July, 1994.

10 February, 1996. "Taking it all Away". *BC Wild*.

11 Interview with Gail Brewer, Ministry of Forests, May, 1998.

12 Letter to Lax Skiik from Fred Philpott and L.A. Hobenshield, July 21, 1992.

13 Letter to Fred Philpott from Leonard Vanderstar, March 16, 1994.

14 Letter to L.A. Hobenshield from Bill Fell, May 1, 1994.

15 Letter to Fred Philpott from George Burns, June 22, 1994.

16 Letter to George Burns from Fred Philpott, September 9, 1998.

17 Letter to Larry Pedersen, from Fred Philpott, April 24, 1995.

18 "Too few trees to keep lifeblood flowing," *The Vancouver Sun*, p.H3, July 11, 1992.

19 Ibid.

20 Letter to Wolfgang Oberresi, from the hereditary chiefs of the Heiltsuk Nation, February 27, 1998.

21 Letter to Arlene Wilson, from the hereditary chiefs of the Heiltsuk Nation, February 11, 1998.

22 G.E. Bridges & Associates Inc. March, 1997. "Strategic Assessment of British Columbia's Northwest Timber Processing Facility, for Forest Renewal BC."

23 Ibid, p.18.

MAP 3.1 Watershed status

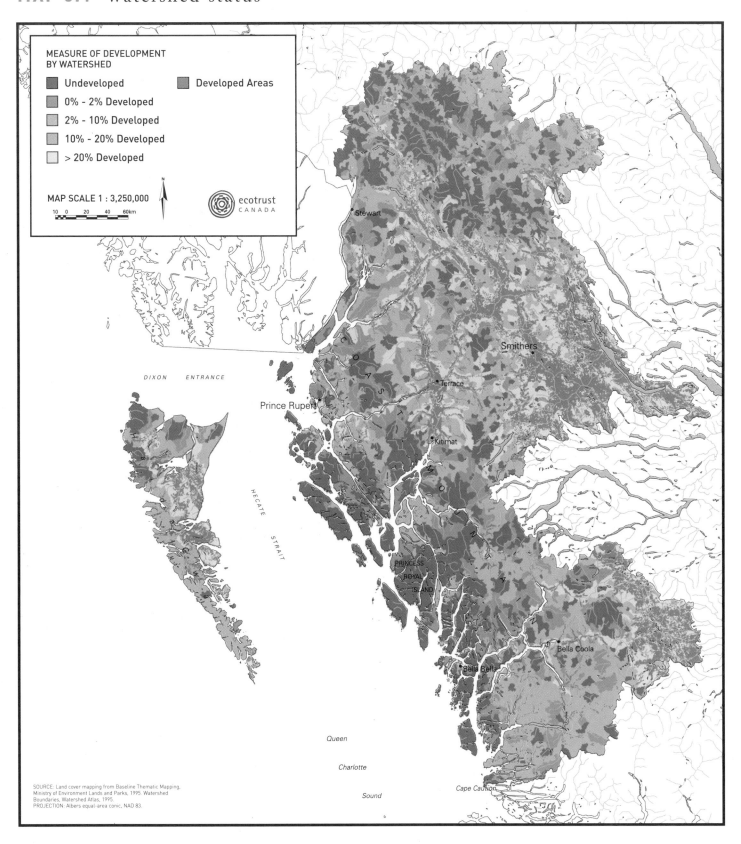

MEASURE OF DEVELOPMENT
BY WATERSHED

- Undeveloped
- 0% – 2% Developed
- 2% – 10% Developed
- 10% – 20% Developed
- > 20% Developed
- Developed Areas

MAP SCALE 1 : 3,250,000

10 0 20 40 60km

ecotrust
CANADA

Stewart

Smithers

Terrace

Prince Rupert

Kitimat

DIXON ENTRANCE

HECATE

STRAIT

PRINCESS
ROYAL
ISLAND

COAST

MOUNTAINS

Bella Coola

Bella Bella

Queen

Charlotte

Sound

Cape Caution

SOURCE: Land cover mapping from Baseline Thematic Mapping,
Ministry of Environment Lands and Parks, 1995. Watershed
Boundaries, Watershed Atlas, 1995.
PROJECTION: Albers equal-area conic, NAD 83.

MAP 3.2a Historic distribution of sawmills

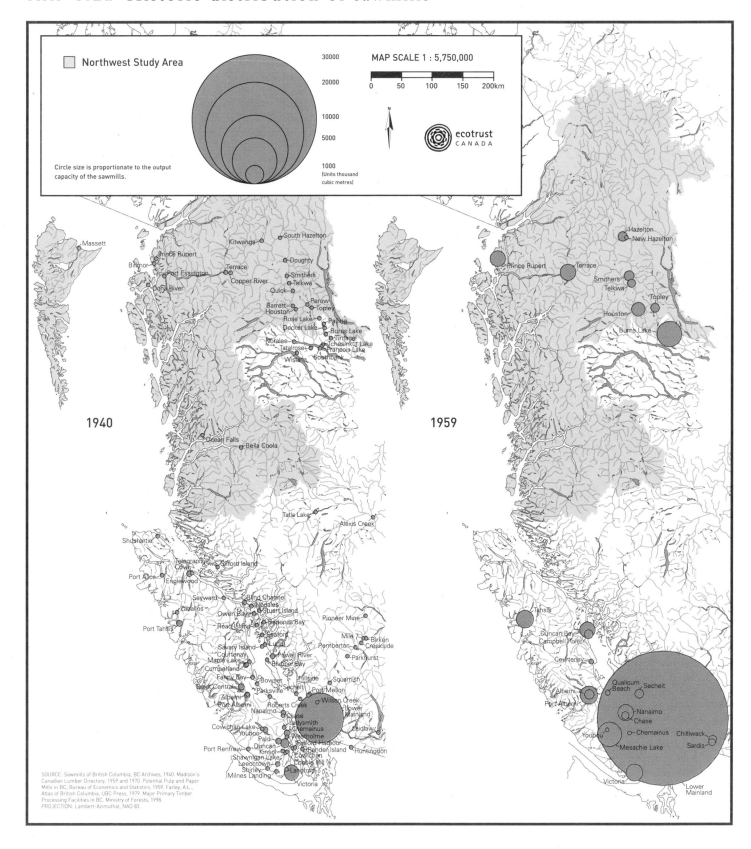

Northwest Study Area

MAP SCALE 1 : 5,750,000

30000
20000
10000
5000
1000 (Units thousand cubic metres)

0 50 100 150 200km

ecotrust CANADA

Circle size is proportionate to the output capacity of the sawmills.

1940

Massett
Kitwanga
South Hazelton
Prince Rupert
Bittimor
Doughty
Port Essington
Terrace
Smithers
Dona River
Copper River
Telkwa
Quick
Perow
Barrett-
Houston
Topley
Rose Lake
Paling
Decker Lake
Burns Lake
Tintagel
Noralee
Tchesinkut Lake
Tatalrose
Francois Lake
Wistaria
Southbank

Ocean Falls
Bella Coola

Tatla Lake
Alexis Creek

Shushartie
Telegraph Cove
Gilford Island
Port Alice
Englewood
Sayward
Blind Channel
Zaballos
Nodales
Stuart Island
Owen Bay
Redonda Bay
Port Tahsis
Read Island
Pioneer Mine
Seaford
Mile 7
Birken
Lund
Creekside
Savary Island
Pemberton
Courtenay
Powell River
Parkhurst
Maple Lake
Blubber Bay
Cumberland
Fanny Bay
Bowser
Hillside
Squamish
Great Central
Sechelt
Parksville
Port Mellon
Alberni
Wilson Creek
Port Alberni
Roberts Creek
Lower
Nanaimo
Mainland
Chase
Leidlaw
Cowichan Lake
Ladysmith
Chemainus
Youbou
Westholme
Paldi
Gifford Harbour
Port Renfrew
Duncan
Pender Island
Huntingdon
Kinsol
Cowichan
Shawnigan Lake
Leechtown
Shirley
Langford
Milnes Landing
Victoria

SOURCE: Sawmills of British Columbia, BC Archives, 1940. Madison's
Canadian Lumber Directory, 1959 and 1970. Potential Pulp and Paper
Mills in BC, Bureau of Economics and Statistics, 1959. Farley, A.L.,
Atlas of British Columbia, UBC Press, 1979. Major Primary Timber
Processing Facilities in BC, Ministry of Forests, 1998.
PROJECTION: Lambert-Azimuthal, NAD 83.

1959

Hazelton
New Hazelton
Prince Rupert
Terrace
Smithers
Telkwa
Topley
Houston
Burns Lake

Tahsis
Duncan Bay
Campbell River
Courtenay
Qualicum
Beach
Sechelt
Alberni
Port Alberni
Nanaimo
Chase
Chemainus
Youbou
Chilliwack
Mesachie Lake
Sardis
Victoria
Lower
Mainland

MAP 3.2b Historic distribution of sawmills

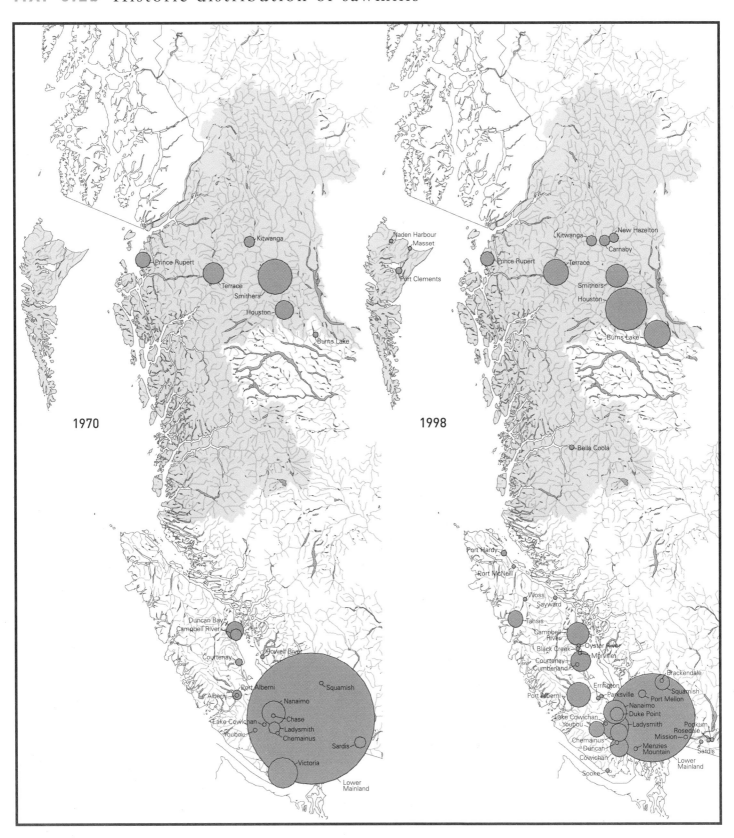

1970

1998

MAP 3.3a Historic vs present day pulp and paper mills

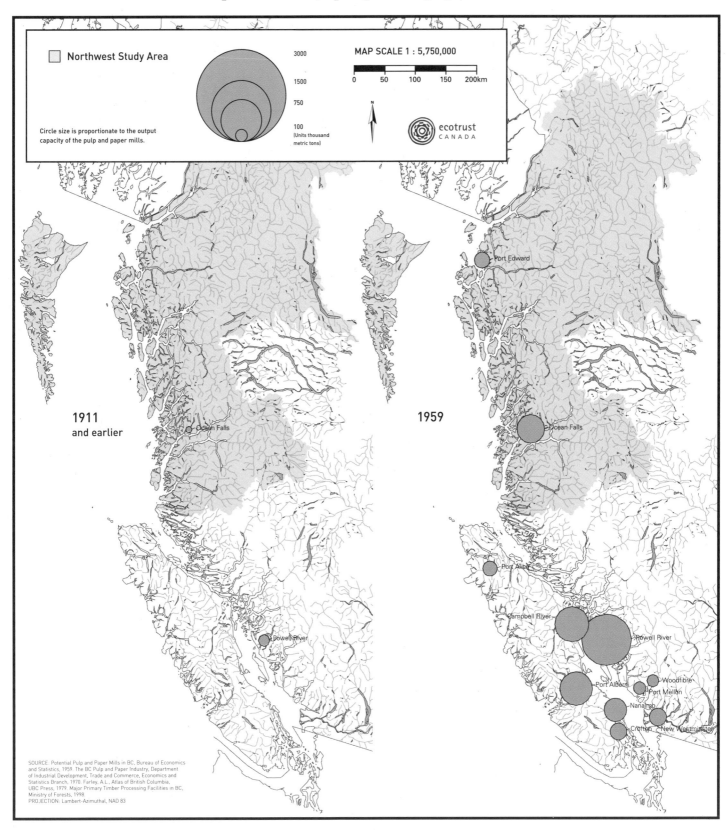

Northwest Study Area

Circle size is proportionate to the output capacity of the pulp and paper mills.

3000
1500
750
100
(Units thousand metric tons)

MAP SCALE 1 : 5,750,000

0   50   100   150   200km

N

ecotrust
CANADA

1911
and earlier

Ocean Falls

Powell River

1959

Port Edward

Ocean Falls

Port Alice

Campbell River

Powell River

Port Alberni

Woodfibre

Port Mellon

Nanaimo

Crofton   New Westminster

SOURCE: Potential Pulp and Paper Mills in BC, Bureau of Economics and Statistics, 1959. The BC Pulp and Paper Industry, Department of Industrial Development, Trade and Commerce, Economics and Statistics Branch, 1970. Farley, A.L., Atlas of British Columbia, UBC Press, 1979. Major Primary Timber Processing Facilities in BC, Ministry of Forests, 1998.
PROJECTION: Lambert-Azimuthal, NAD 83

MAP 3.3b Historic vs present day pulp and paper mills

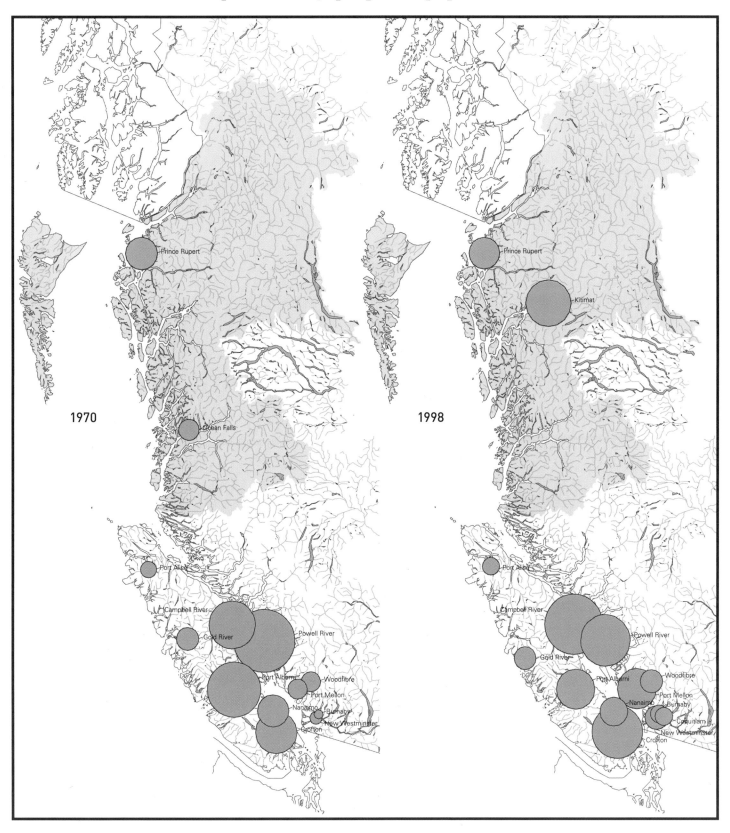

MAP 3.4 Overcut in British Columbia, based on TSA and TFL data

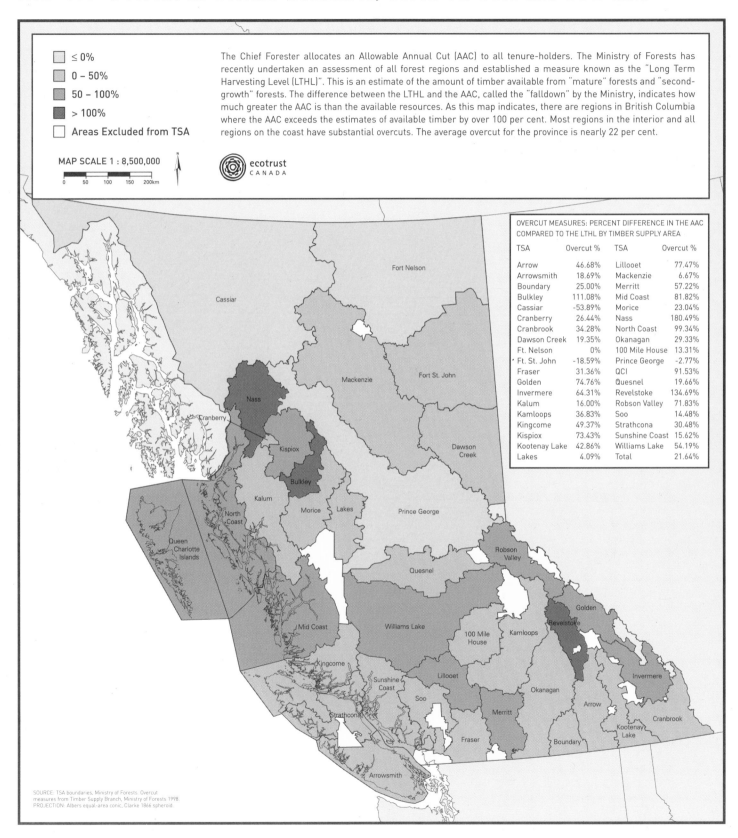

☐	≤ 0%
☐	0 – 50%
☐	50 – 100%
☐	> 100%
☐	Areas Excluded from TSA

MAP SCALE 1 : 8,500,000

0   50   100   150   200km

ecotrust CANADA

The Chief Forester allocates an Allowable Annual Cut (AAC) to all tenure-holders. The Ministry of Forests has recently undertaken an assessment of all forest regions and established a measure known as the "Long Term Harvesting Level (LTHL)". This is an estimate of the amount of timber available from "mature" forests and "second-growth" forests. The difference between the LTHL and the AAC, called the "falldown" by the Ministry, indicates how much greater the AAC is than the available resources. As this map indicates, there are regions in British Columbia where the AAC exceeds the estimates of available timber by over 100 per cent. Most regions in the interior and all regions on the coast have substantial overcuts. The average overcut for the province is nearly 22 per cent.

OVERCUT MEASURES: PERCENT DIFFERENCE IN THE AAC COMPARED TO THE LTHL BY TIMBER SUPPLY AREA

TSA	Overcut %	TSA	Overcut %
Arrow	46.68%	Lillooet	77.47%
Arrowsmith	18.69%	Mackenzie	6.67%
Boundary	25.00%	Merritt	57.22%
Bulkley	111.08%	Mid Coast	81.82%
Cassiar	-53.89%	Morice	23.04%
Cranberry	26.44%	Nass	180.49%
Cranbrook	34.28%	North Coast	99.34%
Dawson Creek	19.35%	Okanagan	29.33%
Ft. Nelson	0%	100 Mile House	13.31%
Ft. St. John	-18.59%	Prince George	-2.77%
Fraser	31.36%	QCI	91.53%
Golden	74.76%	Quesnel	19.66%
Invermere	64.31%	Revelstoke	134.69%
Kalum	16.00%	Robson Valley	71.83%
Kamloops	36.83%	Soo	14.48%
Kingcome	49.37%	Strathcona	30.48%
Kispiox	73.43%	Sunshine Coast	15.62%
Kootenay Lake	42.86%	Williams Lake	54.19%
Lakes	4.09%	Total	21.64%

SOURCE: TSA boundaries, Ministry of Forests. Overcut measures from Timber Supply Branch, Ministry of Forests 1998.
PROJECTION: Albers equal-area conic, Clarke 1866 spheroid.

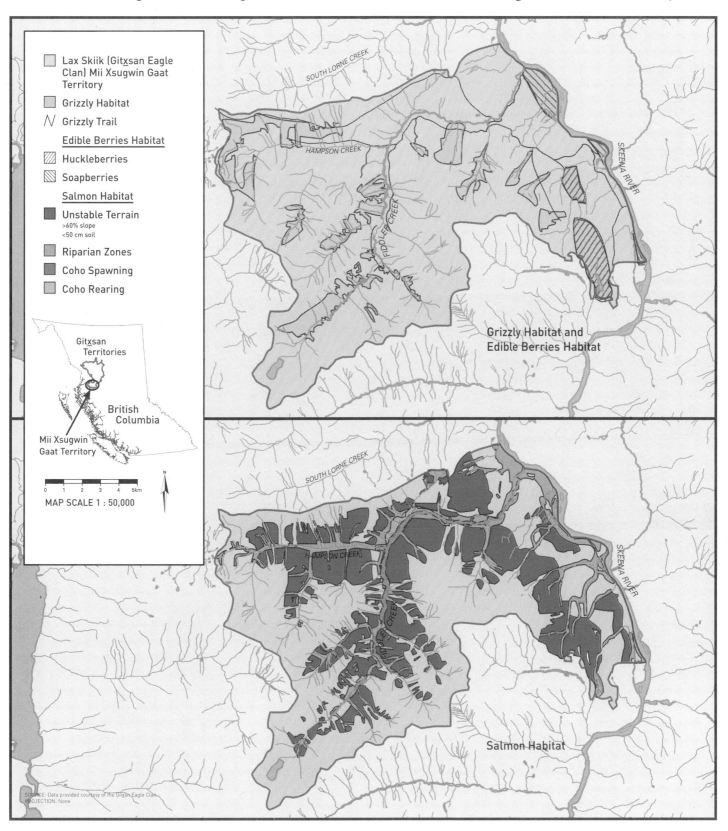

Legend:

- Lax Skiik (Git<u>x</u>san Eagle Clan) Mii Xsugwin Gaat Territory
- Grizzly Habitat
- Grizzly Trail

Edible Berries Habitat
- Huckleberries
- Soapberries

Salmon Habitat
- Unstable Terrain
  >60% slope
  <50 cm soil
- Riparian Zones
- Coho Spawning
- Coho Rearing

Git<u>x</u>san Territories
British Columbia
Mii Xsugwin Gaat Territory

0 1 2 3 4 5km
MAP SCALE 1 : 50,000
N

SOUTH LORNE CREEK
HAMPSON CREEK
FIDDLER CREEK
SKEENA RIVER

Grizzly Habitat and Edible Berries Habitat

Salmon Habitat

SOURCE: Data provided courtesy of the Git<u>x</u>san Eagle Clan
PROJECTION: None

Chapter	# Diversity
4	*By Alex Rose*

NEAR THE MOUTH OF THE KHUTZEYMATEEN, THE FLOATPLANE BEGINS ITS DESCENT. SPOOKED BY our engines, a pod of killer whales dives into the mint green waters of the estuary. Minutes later, we skim into Somerville Inlet where Wilp Syoon – the upscale floating sportfish lodge owned and operated by the Nisga'a Tribal Council – bobs gently in the current.

The pilot cuts the engine; a sudden quiet adds an empyrean quality to a seascape bordered to the east by the Western Kitimat Range of the Coast Mountains.

Waiting dockside is Jim Adams, chief financial officer for the Nisga'a Tribal Council and proud host to an enterprise tailored to a well-heeled international clientele. Behind him, tethered to the wharf are four 21-foot Boston Whalers – each with a 200-horsepower Mercury outboard – used by Nisga'a guides to ferry clients out to the sportfishing grounds.

The summer has been a good one at Wilp Syoon (House of Fishing in the Nisga'a language), Adams explains, ushering us inside for cold beer and plates of fresh-caught Dungeness crab prepared in the lodge's stainless steel kitchen by Nisga'a cook Moses McKay.

Typically, guests pay $2,495 for a five-day, four-night package that includes airfare to and from Vancouver. This summer, the lodge's seven double-occupancy rooms have been booked 75 per cent of the time. Patrons – mostly American and German – are heading back home with crates of wild salmon. Although the lodge makes no guarantees, most anglers "limit out."

Now in the third of a five-year business plan, the lodge is on course to be self-sustaining. But it hasn't been smooth sailing. "Like any new ecotourism initiative, we've had our share of growing pains," Adams explained. "We made mistakes and may

Dennis Nyce, a Nisga'a dancer and carver represents *Naxnok*, Nisga'a Spirit Being, in a traditional dance.
GARY FIEGEHEN

have been victims of our own hubris – the build-it-and-they-will-come syndrome. We realized we needed a tighter business plan and more focused marketing. That's why, earlier this year, we restructured the lodge as a limited company held in trust by the tribal council."

Just before dinner, the first of the fishing parties returns. Two men – a Redmond, Washington software engineer and his son – scramble out of the runabout with lop-sided grins and three silver chinook salmon, one weighing 29 pounds. Sunburnt and giddy with their success, they promise a round for the house as they recap the story of their conquest. The fish had been caught near the mouth of the Nass River; two of the chinook had been hooked and landed by noon; the biggest caught late in the afternoon.

As the other guests return with fish and fishy stories, cook McKay serves plates of smoked sockeye and grilled coho, along with fresh vegetables. Conversation grows expansive. The software engineer tells of 14-hour days and the stress of balancing

career and family; he is thrilled to learn that, although Wilp Syoon has a satellite telephone, there is no email, no voice mail and no digital paging in a place far beyond the range of even the most wired technologies. Dessert and coffee follow; the lodge rocks gently in the current as evening unfolds. Cook McKay is asked about his tribe, its new treaty and its ancient oral tradition.

He speaks of how, across a vast expanse of time, the boundaries between human and animal, light and dark, were transitory and ephemeral.

Nisga'a oral history dates beyond recorded time – to a flood when the glaciers of the last Ice Age were melting. To a time when a frightened, hungry people lashed themselves to mountaintops. To a time when Txeemsim (Clem-sum) – trickster, miracle worker and pivotal figure of Nisga'a cosmology – came down from his sky home to do the bidding of K'amligihahlhaahl or Chief of Heavens.

When Txeemsim first appeared on earth, people lived in twilight, disorder and the constant threat of starvation. Even Txeemsim, Supernatural Being who assumed human and animal forms, had to learn to survive and share with others. Like the Greek god Prometheus, he stole the fire of heaven and brought it back to earth; back to a people huddled in a forbidding, frozen landscape.

Txeemsim's moral dilemmas recall a time when human society, organized in small tribal groups, fought for its very survival. Like the gods of Greek mythology, the Naxnok or spirit beings of this ancient world were manifestations of human hopes and fears. Txeemsim played the role of "transformer," similar to the coyote trickster of the Navajo and the raven of Haida myth. Possessing a keen sense of humor, he was also thief, trickster and liar.

But he also brought the oolichan to the Nass River and, to protect fishing grounds from enemies such as the Haida and Tsimshian, he hurled a mountain into the channel and molded the channels of river so that more salmon would spawn. As McKay explained it, the ancient gods proved that every single action or decision is a moral one, that selfish behavior is ultimately destructive to self and society. One legend, McKay explained, stands as a cautionary tale for contemporary society: protect the earth's ecosystems or perish.

"A long time ago, young people began to ignore the warnings of their elders. They would kill animals needlessly and began to do the same with the fish they caught, maiming them and throwing them back in the lake. Now, in those days, animals, fish and birds were known to have supernatural powers and so the elders lived in constant dread of the catastrophe they knew would happen," McKay explained.

"One day it began to rain. Soon all the waters rose and covered the world. Many people perished. Among these people there was an old woman who had an only daughter.

"'This is the great catastrophe that we have been expecting,' said the old woman to her daughter. 'It has been caused by the thoughtlessness of our young people, and as you were always mindful of what I said, I am going to save you while I can. The others shall be destroyed because the waters are continually rising.'" As legend tells it, the old woman and her daughter were among a handful of people who survived the flood.

Besides being a storehouse of mythic stories, the ancient oral code known as *Ayuukhl Nisga'a* is a sophisticated set of laws that establishes and defines Nisga'a institutions and code of conduct. Under the code, every Nisga'a belongs to a wilp or house which owns its songs, crests, dances, stories and territory. Rights are handed down through matrilineal succession in a ceremony known as the Settlement Feast. Like a deed in a land registry office, the Settlement Feast is a formal registration of title and ownership.

Totally oral, these stories retain a solid base in ritual and are enlivened with each performance – there is no fixed or authoritative version; they change in nuance. Often accompanied by songs and dances, they scintillate with humanity, life and the power of faith and imagination.

Many of the stories are about salmon. During the annual salmon ceremonies, shamans used their extraordinary powers to communicate with the salmon spirits – petitioning the mighty fish to return, once again, to fishing grounds up and down the river.

Tonight, back at the fishing lodge, an ancient tale signals a new beginning. "Under the Nisga'a treaty, we have the legal right – and responsibility – to protect and manage our salmon stocks. We built our own fishwheel and use selective fishing so the salmon will come back forever."

One legend, McKay explained, stands as a cautionary tale for contemporary society: protect the earth's ecosystems or perish

Twenty minutes south by floatplane, the Prince Rupert civic centre is host to a special feast known as *Aadmsteti*. One unseasonably hot summer night, aboriginal people have come to celebrate the weaving of the "nettle net" – the first natural, hand-crafted fishing net produced in the past 60 years. Traditional nets such as this had fallen into disuse as aboriginal fishers began to use European technology. "Sixty-five years ago, my father used a linen net," explained Frances Jackson, who was honoured during the feast. "Then came nylon nets, electronic depth finders and million-dollar seiners."

Proudly showcased at the front of the hall, the nettle net has been intricately and painstakingly hand-woven from the common stinging nettle – the ubiquitous plant found on roadsides throughout the northwest. The construction of the 6 by 18 foot net – with its hand-carved, salmon-shaped wooden floats and grooved granite weights – took almost a year. Every aspect of its manufacture had to be relearned; there were many false starts and weeks of lost time during the rediscovery of a tradition few could remember.

One summer, Jackson and a team of helpers spent six weeks picking more than 18,000 stinging nettle stalks. Then followed a winter of intensive, finger-cramping toil: Once dried, the stalks had to be stripped of their nettles by hand and meticulously woven into thin rope-like strands, which were eventually tied together in 2 by 2 inch sections. An arduous task, weaving the nettle net provided important insight into a traditional skill.

"It was hard work. But once we got started we weren't going to quit," Jackson said. "By weaving the nettle net we want to show our young people to be proud of the past; we want our traditions to stay alive."

Also honoured for her contribution to the net project was Haida artist Frieda Diesing, affectionately known as the "mother of all carvers" to a generation of northwest coast carvers. Born in 1925, Diesing hails from the Haida Eagle clan and belongs to the House of Wehae in Masset. Now in her seventies – a tiny, revving engine of a woman with trim white hair – she has driven to the feast from home in Terrace earlier today, successfully navigating the switchbacks along the Skeena mudflats of Highway 16.

Years ago Diesing had been one of the first carvers to attend the now famous Gitanmaax Carving School at Hazelton. Today, her carvings draw high praise and high prices in galleries around the world. Along with Robert Davidson, Norman Tait, Henry Green and Dempsey Bob, she helped to spark a renaissance of First Nations art and culture that continues to this day, part of a recovery from a century of despair and cultural decimation during which many First Nations artifacts were destroyed, stolen or traded by the missionary men.

The despair began in the heyday of anthropological collecting on the northwest coast, the time between 1875 and the Great Depression when missionaries traveled to aboriginal villages along the British Columbia coast to spread the word of Christ.

The scramble for aboriginal artifacts went on until it seemed that almost everything not nailed down or hidden was gone. The period of most intense collecting coincided with the growth of anthropological museums such as the Smithsonian Institution, the American Museum of Natural

Traditional stinging nettle fishing net – the first produced in the last 60 years – displayed in the Prince Rupert Museum between community project organizers Frances Jackson and Frieda Diesing.
WENDY MANCHUR

History, Chicago's Field Museum of Natural History, the Royal British Columbia Museum and the Canadian Museum of Civilization, to name just a few.

In the late 19th century, Methodist and Anglican missions had already been established in aboriginal villages. By the 1880s, the government of Canada used its authority to assume control over aboriginal people by entering into a partnership with the Christian churches. Missionaries and federal Indian agents came to regard the resistance of the clans and the house chiefs as the most serious impediment in their efforts to convert and "civilize the savages."

North of Cape Caution, First Nations had already been dealing with white explorers and fur traders for several decades. Pragmatic traders themselves, the aboriginal people had, from first contact, shown a willingness to borrow and share with foreign cultures. But as the churchmen set up their missions near aboriginal villages, they introduced a harsh, new order with little room for compromise: accept the terms of a new religion or face eternal damnation.

Many First Nations who converted to Christianity were coerced into giving up their rattles, headdresses, ritual pipes, canoes, baskets, masks and totem poles. Sometimes the pieces were burned. Often, missionaries sold the artifacts to traders who in turn sold them to museums around the world.

Not all artifact collecting was illicit, however. In his book, *Captured Heritage: The Scramble for Northwest Coast Artifacts*, Douglas Cole writes that many aboriginal people voluntarily took part in the frenzied west coast artifact market of the late 1800s and early 1900s. As tokens of respect, some openly gave presents to some early European missionaries, lawyers, Indian agents and anthropologists.

Today, many First Nations are pressing museums, governments and private collectors for the return of the artifacts. So too the church, though recent church decisions add to a climate of mistrust. In 1993, the Anglican Church returned five Nisga'a artifacts, including a mask and shaman's apron, to the Nisga'a people – but only after backing down

when a plan to sell the artifacts (then valued at $300,000) to pay for church renovations infuriated tribal leaders. Now, as stipulated in the Nisga'a treaty, the Royal British Columbia Museum and the Canadian Museum of Civilization will return 300 artifacts and sacred objects which one day will be shown to tourists in a museum planned for Nisga'a territory.

Nine nautical miles to the west of Prince Rupert lies Pike Island, home to three ancient Tsimshian villages. The route – 30 minutes by water taxi – takes us through Venn Passage, the protected sea lane that links Prince Rupert to the Queen Charlottes. On our approach, the sun glints off a stainless steel wharf with cantilevered steps which escalate visitors to the forest floor.

Here in this small green triangle, the Metlakatla First Nation offers a unique heritage tourism experience that resonates with a history from long before European contact. In summer, tourists from around the world, eager to learn about traditional aboriginal cultures, are arriving at Pike Island in increasing numbers.

Traditionally crafted bracelets. During the late 19th century First Nations artifacts were taken and scattered to museums all over the world. The resurgence in their culture and heritage has prompted many First Nations to find and request the return of their rightful belongings.
GARY FIEGEHEN

The scramble for aboriginal artifacts went on until it seemed that almost everything not nailed down or hidden was gone

Today, 14 people – including four female professors from the Netherlands – have each paid $42 for the four-hour cultural experience.

As we are soon to learn, these narrow saltwater passages once harboured the greatest concentration of people in North America north of Mexico. Where now only one Tsimshian village exists (Metlakatla, pop. 153) historians estimate about 8,000 lived in more than 60 villages.

Our tour guide is Charlene MacLean, deputy chief of the nearby Metlakatla First Nation. Here, a series of archaeological digs, or middens, tell the story of an ancient Tsimshian village.

Pike Island measures about 550 by 350 metres; the southern portion is low and flat, the more rugged northern promontory rises to a large bedrock outcrop 20 metres above sea level. Hand-logged years ago, the island is now covered with second-growth western hemlock, Sitka spruce, western red cedar and yellow cedar. At low tide, the pebbled beach forms a bridge to nearby Digby and Shrub Islands.

Saltwater flats attract large flocks of Canada geese and bald eagles nest in the trees. At low tide, MacLean says, a solitary wolf picks its way along the shoreline.

In the intertidal zone, MacLean wets her finger in the sea to trace the shape of an eroded petroglyph. There are two petroglyph sites on the island. One includes dozens of figures on bedrock outcrops scattered along the beach. While most are simple faces, several of the rock carvings are more elaborate. Faded after centuries of tidal action, the stone faces recall the early 20th century geometries of European painter Paul Klee and the surrealist school. One suggests a crab with outstretched legs.

On Pike Island, one ancient village site is in pristine condition with 23 rectangular house depressions arranged in two rows. A series of paths leading from the beach to the village are also visible in the front edge of the midden. Together, these features provide a vivid impression of life thousands of years before Christ.

According to MacLean, oral narratives describe a time of intense warfare between Coast Tsimshian and Tlingit groups, resulting in a general abandonment of the Prince Rupert area. The Coast Tsimshian retreated up the Skeena River as Prince Rupert Harbour became a war zone. Eventually, the Tsimshian people returned and have lived here ever since.

None of these early sites were reoccupied, because the returning Coast Tsimshian adopted a different settlement pattern, locating their villages along the shores of Venn Passage. Later, the area was home to one of the most curious – some say cruel – social experiments in the annals of British Columbia history.

In 1857, to convert the "heathens," Anglican missionary William Duncan had "the gigantic audacity to move uninvited into Tsimshian territory in order to spread the word of a European God." But that is precisely what the English churchman did when, soon after arriving in Victoria, he asked Governor James Douglas for permission to travel to Port

In summer, tourists from around the world, eager to learn about traditional aboriginal cultures, are arriving at Pike Island in increasing numbers

Charlene MacLean, Metlakatla tour guide, teaches tourists about her traditional culture on Pike Island. ALEX ROSE

Simpson and live in the fort until he learned the Tsimshian language. Douglas reluctantly agreed and a few months later, Duncan sailed north on the *Otter*. He found some 2,300 aboriginal people living outside the fort in 140 houses.

Eight months later, Duncan preached his first sermon in Tsimshian, repeating it nine times in nine different houses. He found converts, but he also met resistance and hostility. As Wilson Duff describes it in his standard reference, *The Indian History of British Columbia*, Duncan entered into a test of wills with chiefs who saw no reason to give up their traditional customs and rituals. Year after year, in church and school, Duncan urged his flock to reject their traditional spiritual beliefs and join the Christian church.

By 1859 he decided it was necessary to move his converts and establish a Christian village at Metlakatla, where the Tsimshian made their winter home. The move was made in 1862, just as the first news of the great smallpox epidemic came from Victoria; his converts escaped the disease while nearby "heathen" Fort Simpson was hit hard.

At Metlakatla, the churchman created a "model Christian, self-supporting industrial mission." To live there, aboriginal people had to conform to 15 laws of conduct, which required them to give up many features of their old life – dancing, potlatching, shamanism and the like. They also had to take religious instruction, observe the Sabbath, send their children to school, build neat houses and pay a village tax. In this "New Jerusalem" all rank and class were abolished, incredibly – since the Tsimshian had one of the most elaborate class systems on the northwest coast.

Metlakatla made a profound impression on Indian Commissioner I. W. Powell when he made his first tour of inspection in 1879. He found Duncan presiding over "one of the most orderly, respectable and industrious communities to be found in any Christian country." Its population was then about 1,100. In dress, speech and conduct the people were outstanding. Their houses were uniform, 18 by 36 feet, with two rooms downstairs and

three bedrooms up with fenced gardens. The church was large enough to seat 800, the school 500. A sawmill cut all the lumber used in the village; there was also a sash factory, blacksmith shop, bakery, weaving house and trading post. Plans were being made for a salmon cannery and brickyard, which were later completed.

All this was controlled and created by Duncan, who explained in a later letter to Powell, "The men were divided – by drawing lots – into ten companies. Each company had a headman, two elected elders, two constables, three councillors and 10 firemen with a captain. The village tax was three dollars or one week's labour a year." The dissension that was to divide and destroy this "model" community began in 1879 when northern British Columbia was made the Diocese of Columbia and Bishop William Ridley was sent to take charge of Metlakatla. Ridley and Duncan were men of strong character with strong views on religion. Ridley, for example, wanted to introduce the orthodox ritual of the High Church, but Duncan, a layman, thought it would be misinterpreted by the aboriginal people. The Bishop's high station in the church was matched by Duncan's secure place in the community. The villagers were troubled witnesses to the conflict, later taking sides as they were drawn into it themselves. In the end, Ridley had Duncan relieved of his post and the missionary returned to Victoria.

But Duncan wasn't finished. After a trip to Washington to clear the way, he moved in 1887 to Annette Island in Alaska to create a new and even better Metlakatla. Of the 948 people left in the original community, 823 eventually followed him to Alaska.

Duncan and other churchmen left behind a complicated and painful legacy that smoulders to this day. On the one hand, many aboriginal people

Many church leaders played an important role in the struggle for aboriginal rights. On the other hand, the Church served as the advance guard for a cultural blitzkrieg that would destroy a way of life for many.

The churchmen viewed sacred totem poles and others objects as "evil" – competing directly with the Christian cross

Totems at Gitanyou (Kitwanga), Skeena River. Many significant cultural artifacts were considered to be works of evil by Christian missionaries. First Nations were discouraged from creating and using their sacred objects.
B.C. ARCHIVES, # I-15825

were eager to join the new church and, as any dispassionate reading of British Columbia history must conclude, many church leaders were progressives who, like modern-day activists, played an important role in the struggle for aboriginal rights.

On the other hand, the church served as the advance guard for a cultural blitzkrieg that would soon destroy a way of life for many. First efforts were to despoil, cheapen and mock the cosmology and spirituality of the aboriginal people they met and preached among. Misunderstanding from the start, the churchmen viewed sacred totem poles and others objects as "evil" – competing directly with the Christian cross.

Politicians were no better. It was 1887 when British Columbia Premier William Smithe met a contingent of Nisga'a and other northwest coast First Nations who had arrived in Victoria's inner harbour to settle the Land Question. Smithe's message was blunt: "When the white man first came among you, you were little better than the wild beasts of the field."

Even as this brutal racism was translated into narrow policies which plunged the country into a century of darkness for aboriginal people, more was soon to come. In 1913, Duncan Campell Scott became deputy superintendent of Indian Affairs. His vision, later codified as the Indian Act, would dominate federal aboriginal policy for decades. "I want to get rid of the Indian problem," Mr. Scott wrote. "Our objective is to continue until there is not a single Indian in Canada that has not been absorbed into the body politic and there is no Indian question."

And so it was. Throughout the 20th century a series of government policies – supported by the Christian churches – worked to decimate every aspect of aboriginal culture. The systemic destruction of languages, spiritual beliefs, customs, family structure and art led many First Nations to the precipice of extinction, with residential schools providing the coup de grace – teaching generations of First Nations to despise and reject their traditional cultures.

The task of revitalizing a culture obliterated by a century of government- and church-sanctioned assimilation can only be described as Herculean.

No words can convey the depths of toxic despair and cultural disintegration found in many aboriginal communities today. As cultures die, they are stricken with the mute, implacable rage of that humanity strangled within them. So long as it grows, a culture depends on the elaboration of meaning, its health maintained by an awareness of its state; as it dies, it opens itself up to the fury of those betrayed by its meaning.

Today, Charlene MacLean herds us past the spot where Duncan built his church. A concrete-and-steel structure – the town hall for the Metlakatla First Nation – now graces the site. Here, in the shadow of a failed social experiment, MacLean and other tribal leaders work to take control over their own lives.

Waving goodbye at the dock, MacLean is showered with thanks for her Pike Island tour. After the

tourists depart, she grows quiet, circumspect. "It is one thing to talk about reclaiming a traditional culture," she muses, "but quite another to do something about it."

Thoughtful and self-possessed, MacLean also has a personal story to tell. Recently, she returned to live full-time in this coastal community with her husband and two young children. The mean streets of Vancouver's Downtown Eastside, she explains, were no place to raise a family.

"But there are many, many social problems right here at home. We have to do better at our schools and send more of our kids to post secondary. Perhaps, most of all, we have to stop thinking of ourselves as victims. We have to look back at those aspects of our traditional culture that have to do with independence and power. Then, we have to learn how to use them in today's society."

Today, on the streets of Prince Rupert, many people feel betrayed by an economic system in ruins.

In the shadow of the pulp mill, the city of Prince Rupert lurches from one economic crisis to another. Despite a $350-million bailout from the provincial government, Skeena Cellulose is still hemorrhaging red ink. Across town, the commercial salmon fleet idles at the dock.

Over the past two decades, Prince Rupert has emerged as an unfortunate symbol of a failed Canadian dream. Features in national newspapers document a century of false hopes and broken promises – all planned at cabinet tables in faraway Ottawa and Victoria or corporate boardrooms in New York, Calgary or Tokyo.

The seeds of this failure are rooted deep in colonial history. On the land, European pioneers savaged immense stands of Douglas fir and cedar with a rapacious ferocity unmitigated by any notions of scarcity or conservation. And, out at sea, utilizing the electronics of a modern navy, the commercial fleet, over the past half century, has fished some salmon stocks to the point of near-extinction.

Fuelled by 19th century notions of resource extraction, the city has never lived up to its own advertisements as a superport – despite the promise of a series of vaunted mega projects. First came coal, wheat and liquid natural gas. Today, economic dreams are predicated on vague pronouncements of new aluminum smelters and offshore oil and gas exploration. Meanwhile, over the past two years, some estimate 2,000 people left town (current population is about 17,000), many walking away from bad debts and mortgages.

On the docks, news from the commercial fleet is unrelentingly bad. Several stocks of salmon are now at endangered levels and catches have dropped even more. Compounding the problem, prices for salmon have plummeted. As a result, fishers landed only $55-million in 1998 – less than one quarter of their average earnings in the early 1990s.

The summer of 2000 wasn't any better. Depressed salmon stocks – the result of decades of overfishing, habitat destruction and blatant human greed – are compounded by mysterious changes in ocean temperatures affecting the survival of the salmon at sea, which may be related to worldwide climate changes and global warming.

Tough times may explain why so many residents practice a kind of collective denial – "fishing and logging are cyclical; they are sure to bounce back; just wait for the new oil and gas exploration." Others are hostile and bellicose, lashing out at government officials and policies made "in Ottawa or down south."

Denial, for some, seems absolute. Several years ago, during the acrimonious standoff with the Americans over the Pacific Salmon Treaty, an armada of frustrated Prince Rupert fishers, in a move to restart stalled negotiations, blockaded the U.S. ferry to Alaska. The strategy backfired as the story became international news. As a direct result of the bad press – which in the tourist industry can take

Over the past two decades, Prince Rupert has emerged as an unfortunate symbol of a failed Canadian dream

"When it comes to cultural and adventure tourism, uniqueness and excellence sell. But we can't operate in an environment that has been desecrated"

years, even decades to repair – fewer American tourists are visiting Prince Rupert. And while business at hotels, restaurants and charter operators is down, few people appear willing to acknowledge this cause-and-effect relationship.

Some residents express a nostalgic longing for an earlier, more affluent time when homes in neighbourhoods such as Roosevelt Hill sported two trucks and a powerboat. Many reference the more affluent 50s or 60s when the pulp mill operated at full shift and seine boat skippers, returning to port loaded with sockeye or herring roe, bought endless rounds in the city's many pubs.

While the city is now making a series of latter-day efforts to address its economic malaise, most of Prince Rupert's important economic decisions are still made elsewhere. And, as an old-style industrial economy heavily dependent on natural resource extraction, Prince Rupert can hardly compete with the new high-tech economies of Vancouver, Seattle or Portland.

A small group of self-activating people, however, refuse to play the blame game or succumb to a culture of despair. Accepting and understanding the structural causes of the harsh new economic reality has ushered in a time of critical self reflection. Some are asking big questions about the economy and their jobs; at the same time they are beginning to examine their own culture and its historical relationship with its aboriginal neighbours.

Indeed, apparently unnoticed by city leaders, Prince Rupert has become a kind of working laboratory for a racially integrated society – a prototype for a place where aboriginal and non-aboriginal people work and live together. Visitors to Prince Rupert can see this for themselves.

The streets teem with the faces of a dozen tribal groups; young aboriginal women wheel baby strollers past people whose ancestors came from Scotland, Norway and China. Prince Rupert has

created something special – a cohesiveness evinced by a century of interracial marriage.

But this human potential seems lost on those who appear to have little interest in a new generation of First Nations and civic entrepreneurs. A planned seawall walk – loaded with tourism potential – proceeds at a glacial pace as the city and the Canadian National Railway wrangle over jurisdiction. As a result, the area remains an unmitigated planning disaster where a long line of empty canneries obliterates the harbour view.

Accessible only by boat, plane or ferry, Bella Bella is mid-point on the B.C. coast. Here, where fjords slice into the basalt of steep mountains, Heiltsuk entrepreneurs Frank and Kathy Brown launched a heritage-based ecotourism company back in 1996. Since then, about 15,000 tourists have taken one of several guided tours which all include interpretive commentary.

SeeQuest was quick to capitalize on new opportunities provided by the new provincial ferry that connects Vancouver Island to Bella Coola and other coastal communities. In concert with the B.C. Museum of Anthropology, the company sponsored an oolichan exhibit and "Cannery Days – A Chapter in the Lives of the Heiltsuk." Future plans include the construction of a traditional big house at nearby McLoughlin Bay, which would be the first to be built by the Heiltsuk in 150 years. As well, four new house poles have been carved by local artist Stanley George.

Here in Bella Bella, where ancient petroglyphs stare out over a haunting seascape, the Heiltsuk Nation is hyper-vigilant about the downside of mass tourism. If eco or cultural tourism becomes much more popular, it may ultimately threaten the very things that are good for its business. "It is one thing to support the resurgence of our traditional culture, but if we deplete or destroy our resources, we're going to have to live with the results," explained Frank Brown.

"When it comes to cultural and adventure tourism, uniqueness and excellence sell. But we can't operate in an environment that has been desecrated."

Also emphasizing environmental ethics, another Heiltsuk program teaches a self-reliance that is hard to find in a community paralyzed by a seasonal unemployment rate of more than 80 per cent. The Heiltsuk Dhal Yaci Society was formed to address nothing less than the "wellness of the Heiltsuk people."

"We're reaching out to our aboriginal kids – 16 and older, many who are high-school dropouts," said program manager Larry Jorgenson. "We teach them to work, we teach them self-worth, and we also teach them about the past. By relearning aspects of their traditional culture – especially when it comes to spirituality and healing – they can learn to take care of themselves."

In 1999, with a staff of 12 and an operating budget of $180,000, Jorgenson supervised the construction of five new cabins in the Bella Bella area, for a total of nine. "With the support and encouragement of our traditional chiefs and elders, we hope to rekindle the ties to a territory that sustained us for thousands of years," Jorgenson said, a non-aboriginal who visited Bella Bella 20 years ago and stayed to marry a Heiltsuk woman. Today, the Jorgensons live in Bella Bella with their two children.

"Ours is a sacred place," Jorgenson said, who has a masters degree in community planning. "We must stop the destruction of the forest and marine resources here on Heiltsuk traditional territory." To this end, the Heiltsuk are developing their own conservation program to monitor the activities of logging companies, fishers, hunters and other visitors.

Haisla young people learn traditional dances. Rediscovery programs such as this focus on teaching youth about the history and traditions of First Nations culture.
PARRY MEAD

Bella Bella is also the site of the three Qqs (Heiltsuk for "eyes") summer camp programs for Heiltsuk children. The program offers five and seven nights of supervised overnight camping adventures for children nine to 18.

The cultural rediscovery camps have proved popular: This past summer, 64 children, divided into small groups and supervised by adult guides, paddled canoes into estuaries and inlets, where they set up camp. At night, around the campfires, children played a series of "rediscovery" games, songs and dances.

Haisla Rediscovery camp on the Kitlope River. For many it's the trip of a lifetime.
DYLAN SIMONDS

So far, a total of 139 children have participated in the Qqs summer camps. Most were thrilled, said coordinator Elroy White: "Swimming and fishing are the biggest hits. Late in the afternoon, after we set up camp, we cook dinner over an open campfire – cooking fish the kids have caught during the day. For many, it's an experience of a lifetime."

The Heiltsuk and other First Nations are well-placed to take advantage of new trends in tourism. The World Tourism Organization estimates that nature tourism alone generates seven per cent of all international travel expenditures. While global tourism has been growing at an annual rate of four per cent, nature travel has grown between 10 and 30 per cent in recent years. But it is an already crowded field.

According to the Canadian Tourism Commission, the number of adventure and ecotourism operators in Canada was more than 1,850 in 1999, with revenues of more than $500-million. And many times that amount is spent on outdoor equipment and clothing. In the U.S., some estimates have placed the number of outdoor outfitters at more than 20,000 and adventure-industry revenues are measured in billions of dollars. Analysts predict the trend will grow until the first wave of baby boomers retires.

Time and the marketplace will be the final arbiters when it comes to the economic sustainability of these and myriad other eco and cultural tourism initiatives. Wilp Syoon, SeeQuest and Pike Island have already succeeded in establishing successful companies based on authentic First Nations heritage. In ecotourism, where perceptions can quickly translate into reality, all operators must meet expectations of their visitors – confident that they can measure the degree of satisfaction delivered by the actual experience. And, in a crowded marketplace, where "consumer delight" is a governing benchmark, mere word-of-mouth endorsements can be as handicapping as a blindfolded shadow-boxer.

To some extent, however, the question of long-term business success may be moot. These First Nations entrepreneurs, digging deep into their own roots, have already pointed the way to future conservation-based economic opportunities.

Linking conservation to cultural rediscovery, operations at Wilp Syoon, Pike Island and SeeQuest have incorporated conservation as a core value – built right into their business plans.

By harvesting no more than is replenished naturally and learning to manage natural resources to restore and maintain biological diversity, these and other ventures have shown it is possible to live and work off the land without eroding what Ecotrust Canada describes as "natural capital."

These and many other First Nations entrepreneurs fully understand their cultural and economic survival hinges directly on the protection of this capital. And, by rediscovering and showcasing their traditional cultures – still resonating with mystery and power – to tourists from around the world, they have created prototypes for a new and better way to live and work, here in the rain forests north of Cape Caution.

REFERENCES

1998. "Report on Business." *The Globe and Mail.*

1998. Department of Fisheries and Oceans Statistical Review.

Ames, Kenneth M. and H. Maschner. 1999. *Peoples of the Northwest Coast: Their Archaeology and Prehistory. London:* Thames and Hudson.

Ayuukhl Nisga'a, the ancient Nisga'a oral code of laws.

Berlo, Janet C. and R. Phillips. 1998. *Native North American Art.* New York: Oxford University Press.

Canadian Tourism Commission. 1998. *Adventure Travel and Ecotourism: The Challenge Ahead.*

Cole, Douglas. 1995. *Captured Heritage: The Scramble for Northwest Coast Artifacts.* Vancouver: Douglas and McIntyre.

Duff, Wilson. 1997. *The Indian History of British Columbia: The Impact of the White Man.* British Columbia: Royal British Columbia Museum. 3rd edition.

Holm, Bill. 1965. *Northwest Coast Art: An Analysis of Form.* Seattle: University of Washington Press.

Rose, Alex.1998. *Bringing our Ancestors Home: The Repatriation of Nisga'a Artifacts.* New Aiyanish: Nisga'a Tribal Council.

Rose, Alex.1993. *Nisga'a: People of the Nass River.* Vancouver: Douglas and McIntyre.

People and the Land

By Hilistis (Pauline Waterfall), Doug Hopwood and Ian Gill

The Heiltsuk have creation stories that connect them to specific territories, history, and values. These stories explain how we came to be placed here by our Maker and how our ancestral roots kept us strong and independent as responsible recipients of our Creator's gifts.

The late Heiltsuk Elder, Willie Gladstone, told of how our Maker placed the first man in this part of the world. When he became conscious of his surroundings, he saw only water. So, he went back to sleep and when he awoke, there were rock foundations. He went back to sleep again and awoke this time to find the beginnings of other life forms. The legend goes on to tell of how the Maker created all things in the beginning. The original man was then given a wife and family.

Another legend tells of how a lazy man was excommunicated because of his unwillingness to provide for himself and contribute to the well being of the community. He learned his lessons and, with divine intervention, he assisted in the creation of a new village. The man carved fish forms out of alder wood and placed them into the nearby river, where they came alive and provided a key source of food to sustain the new community.

Then, there were rituals that were conducted to honour the life taken from various sources for provision of food, shelter, transportation and other sustenance needs.

For example, when a man caught the first salmon of the season, he conducted a ceremony that included praying to the spirit of the salmon. He respectfully cleaned and prepared it as if he would be cooking it. Then eagle down was placed on the flesh and the salmon was returned to the waters. An appeal was made for its spirit to return to the extended salmon family with the promise that only what was needed would be taken, and that its life was honoured and vital to support the lives of those who would eat it.

Aerial view of Bella Bella (Waglisla), the main community of the Heiltsuk First Nation and largest First Nation community on the central coast. DAVE NUNUK

The Heiltsuk regard their traditional territory as an extension of their homes. The waters are their highway and pantry. The forests are their pharmacy and garden. The rivers and lakes are their larder. Traditionally, they were responsible stewards of the land and waters, upon which they were dependent for life itself. They knew that actions taken today would impact generations to come. So, each decision was carefully weighed until consensus was reached and reinforced through tribal laws. These laws tied them to the land and waters. They were taught that all life on earth is valuable and vital to sustaining the delicate interdependence, with no life being superior to another. They acknowledged and honoured the spirit of life that was being sacrificed for their benefit in food harvesting, housing, clothing and other sustenance needs. They knew that their extended home reached beyond the boundaries of their houses. They understood that

whatever was done to one part would affect the other. They accepted their responsibility to maintain their homeland and take necessary measures required to reinforce the foundation of this home. Their relationship with the land and waters was so intimate that each creek, river, lake, mountain, rock and other land marks were given a Heiltsuk name. This name usually revealed certain qualities that would indicate the importance of each feature.

This was how it was since time began, and yet, it was to change due to circumstances beyond the Heiltsuk's control. Outsiders arrived, and stayed. In 1913, the Heiltsuk Hemas (hereditary chiefs) had an opportunity to express their concerns when the McKenna-McBride Royal Commission on Indian Affairs for the Province of British Columbia convened in Bella Bella.

"We wish to thank you for your kindness in coming to look into our troubles. There are white

Heiltsuk Hereditary Chiefs in full traditional regalia. First Nations have tremendous respect for the natural environment, knowing that without the water and land, they would not survive and prosper.
IAN MCALLISTER

men coming in here and settling on the land, and we are not able to tell in the first place whether they are bona fide settlers or whether they just squat here to help themselves. We don't visit other places and take up land, and we don't see why other people should come and take ours."

With that, Chief Bob Anderson made it abundantly clear that the Heiltsuk Nation was powerfully opposed to the encroachment of industry and settlers on Heiltsuk land. But Bob Anderson's words went unheeded, the Heiltsuk's concerns were ignored. The McKenna-McBride Commission consigned the Heiltsuk to 2,375 hectares of reserve lands, a tiny fraction of one per cent of their territory, and outsiders got their way with the rest of the territory and have done so ever since.

Today, almost a century later, Chief Bob Anderson's statement still holds true for the Heiltsuk people. In fact, his declaration was revived as the mission statement for the Heiltsuk Treaty Office, and has become a rallying point for Heiltsuk people.

Chief Bob Anderson went on to say: "We know that it is unlawful to steal land, and we have no way of finding out whether these men who come and squat here are proper settlers or not. We are the Natives of this Country and we want all the land we can get. We feel that we own the whole of this Country, every bit of it, and we ought to have something to say about it."

Having "something to say about it" does not imply a warning, or suggest arrogance. Rather, it reflects the Heiltsuk tradition of collectively discussing all matters that required an important decision that was reached by consensus. Open and clear communication was vital to this process so that all could reach an informed consensus, knowing that the impact would have far-reaching implications for generations to come. This was the only way to ensure proper stewardship of the land and waters of Heiltsuk territory.

The Heiltsuk word for the "world" is *waaxwais*. While the Heiltsuk had a global awareness, they were respectful of the territory over which

other original peoples had stewardship. In Hemas Anderson's comments above, his phrase "this Country" refers to the Heiltsuk traditional territory. The Heiltsuk had no jurisdiction over territories outside of their boundaries, nor did they accept that people from outside had jurisdiction over their traditional lands and waters.

Now, after decades of being ignored or drowned out by the demands of so-called stakeholders, the Heiltsuk's voice is once again being heard. The Heiltsuk are working to articulate a vision for their community that transcends short-term political cycles, eschews agenda-driven planning processes, and instead provides a comprehensive, legally defensible, scientifically sound and culturally rich plan that will assure the community of a sustainable future. This time, the Heiltsuk will not be brushed aside.

For thousands of years the Heiltsuk have held detailed local knowledge of the lands and waters that make up their territory, yet their expertise was not considered when policies were created that displaced them from their land and resources. Since the arrival of the first Europeans they have spoken with eloquence and energy in defence of their rights to use the resources of the lands and waters. With equal passion they have spoken against short-sighted over-use or destruction of the ecological fabric that has supported their culture for centuries beyond memory. None of this is new, but in recent years new developments have added strength and clarity to Heiltsuk voices.

On December 11, 1997, the Supreme Court of Canada announced its decision in the *Delgamuukw* case, in which elders of the Gitxsan and Wet'suwet'en Nations of north-central British Columbia appealed an earlier court decision that had denied the existence of aboriginal rights and

> **Chief Bob Anderson made it abundantly clear that the Heiltsuk Nation was powerfully opposed to the encroachment of industry and settlers on Heiltsuk land. But Bob Anderson's words went unheeded, the Heiltsuk's concerns were ignored**

An abandoned cable wire used in old-time logging methods in Nameless Creek. Now buried under logging debris, this small tributary stream was once productive salmon habitat.
MIKE JACOBS

In addition to traditional use data, First Nations must have technical expertise in fisheries, forestry and other resource management fields

title. The *Delgamuukw* decision confirmed the existence of aboriginal title, and specified the need for a consultation process whenever industrial activities are expected to interfere with First Nations opportunities to continue exercising traditional rights. The court noted that whenever infringement of an aboriginal right is contemplated "there is always a duty of consultation" and "some cases may even require the full consent of an Aboriginal nation." The decision also encouraged negotiation rather than litigation relating to Aboriginal rights and title.

The *Delgamuukw* decision is particularly significant in British Columbia where the absence of treaties contributes to uncertainty regarding the ownership and management of lands and resources. But although *Delgamuukw* affirms the existence of aboriginal rights and title, it still places much of the burden of proof for establishing that title on First Nations. First Nations can only hope to prove title

by amassing and presenting detailed and well-researched information about the extent and nature of traditional uses of the land. For this reason, completion of a high-quality study documenting traditional land use and occupancy is an essential step for First Nations to realize the potential given them by *Delgamuukw* to regain control of their traditional lands and resources.

In addition to traditional use data, First Nations must have technical expertise in fisheries, forestry and other resource management fields. Skill in Geographic Information Systems (GIS) is needed to handle large amounts of data about land and resources. When these scientific skills are developed and used in combination with traditional knowledge and perspectives, the two approaches inform and reinforce each other. For the Heiltsuk, an example of the power of this synergy came when a logging company submitted a five-year forest development plan for logging in a Heiltsuk watershed called Nameless Creek.

Heiltsuk elder and retired fisherman Cyril Carpenter looked at the logging plan. Cyril remembered that Nameless Creek used to have large runs of pink and chum salmon, but after logging, sometime around the First World War, the fish runs had declined. That is the kind of detailed local knowledge only found in communities that live close to the land – but such information, often dismissed as anecdotal and unscientific, gets little respect among governments and forest companies. Certainly, it seldom works its way into companies' five-year development plans.

Fortunately, a Heiltsuk stream survey crew was able to visit Nameless Creek to confirm Cyril's information. The crew found chunks of rusty cable embedded in the stream bed, and other evidence indicating that the old-time loggers had used a donkey winch to yard logs down the stream bed, causing serious and long-lasting damage to salmon habitat. Despite this visible evidence, the forest development plan prepared by the company claimed exemption from any requirement to assess the cumulative impact of past and proposed logging on fish habitat in the watershed, stating that there was "no significant history of logging in Nameless Creek." With a combination of local traditional knowledge and rigorous modern survey methods, the Heiltsuk are clearly in possession of more complete and accurate information than either the government or the logging companies, enabling them to speak from a renewed position of authority on matters relating to the land. In the words of Chief Bob Anderson, they "have something to say about it."

It remains to be seen whether the company will revise its logging plans to prevent further damage to fish habitat in Nameless Creek. But there is no doubt that the will of the community has been re-awakened. This renewed awareness, combined with growing technical skills and detailed information, puts the Heiltsuk in a stronger position than ever before to protect the resources of their territory from the ravages of shortsighted exploitation. Nameless Creek is only the beginning. There are a lot of other creeks in Heiltsuk territory, and a lot of forest development plans, current and anticipated. The Heiltsuk intend to have something to say about all of them.

The Heiltsuk Nation's territory encompasses a huge region, nearly four million hectares of land and water. It is home to an extraordinary abundance of natural resources that have sustained the Heiltsuk people for thousands of years, or according to their teaching – since time began. In chapter 2, Terry Glavin has written about Namu, and about the significance of the marine environment for coastal people. The Heiltsuk's was a sophisticated culture sustained by a vigorous and diverse resource economy. Historically, they lived in up to 55 villages, and ranged over their entire territory, marine and terrestrial. Until, that is, they were decimated by disease and forced onto tiny reserves. Today, the Heiltsuk live on just one reserve, at Bella Bella. Today, they are legally confined to about 600 of their almost four million hectares.

Bella Bella is, nonetheless, the largest First Nations community on the central coast. In 1999,

Tourists disembarking a ferry at Bella Bella. Tourism has increased since B.C. Ferries began service to a few small towns along the central coast in 1998, bringing more dollars to the local economy.
SETH ZUCKERMAN

the community's population was 1,442 people, of whom 1,357 were aboriginal and 85 were non-native. A further 800 Heiltsuk people live away from the territory. The resident population peaks in the summer when family members return to the community for traditional food harvesting, social visits or participation in rites of passage. More recently, tourists add to the influx, largely via a ferry service inaugurated in 1998.

Within the next century, the population of the Heiltsuk Nation will increase sixfold, according to a report prepared for the Heiltsuk by Urban Eco Consultants Ltd. That is, a nation whose population currently barely tops 2,000 people will grow to almost 12,000 people. Thus the Heiltsuk, as with so many First Nations communities on the coast, are caught between a dramatically declining resource base, with almost none of the assets from resource extraction remaining in the community, and a rapidly increasing population. "Given the heavy reliance of Bella Bella and Lower Mainland Heiltsuk on traditional resources from [Heiltsuk territory], it is clear [natural] resources must be protected for future generations," says a draft integrated marine and land use plan prepared for the community. "Failure to do so will have a dramatic adverse impact on the cultural integrity of the Heiltsuk Nation, given that traditional marine and terrestrial resource uses define the Heiltsuk Nation's distinct culture."

Indeed, even today, the Heiltsuk continue to use their territory to hunt wildlife, fish, gather and prepare foods and medicines, sell, barter and trade traditional resources, conduct sacred ceremonies, seek spiritual guidance, and live.

Heiltsuk people have always placed the highest priority on conservation and protection of lands and resources, and living in harmony with nature. Traditionally, these values were implemented through a system of tribal laws known as *Gvai'ilas*, which reflected values of respect, honour, caring, sharing, oneness, sacredness and interdependence. The Heiltsuk practiced the custom of *ba-qui-la* where each person was responsible for working hard to collect, prepare and share traditional foods to assure that all were provided for during the long, harsh winter months. With this practice, there were rituals that were conducted to assure that only what was needed was taken. For example, when plants were harvested for medicinal purposes, there were

Heiltsuk science students measure the diameter of an ancient giant spruce tree to learn about forest management and ecological principles, a part of Ecotrust Canada's work in Bella Bella.
DOUG HOPWOOD

Gvai'ilas that included: removing no more than four plants in a specific area, harvesting after the plant's reproduction cycle, cutting only a small square in the tree's bark, and so on.

After the arrival of Europeans, Heiltsuk tribal laws and Chief's authorities were undermined by governmental policies: cultural practices, outlawed; traditional knowledge, discounted; Heiltsuk territory, exploited – to the demise of the Heiltsuk world, and with virtually no benefits flowing to Heiltsuk people. In fact, they were legally displaced from their homeland and a system of sustaining resources was drastically eroded and compromised.

At the end of the 19th century, the first Methodist missionary arrived on the shores of the Heiltsuk village. His vessel was met by the villagers and he told them about his purpose and spiritual beliefs. He asked permission to come and work among them. They asked him to stay offshore until they deliberated with the community members as a whole. This process took place over two days and the missionary's journals indicate how relieved he was to receive his invitation to stay.

The late Hilistis, Beatrice Brown, was asked why the missionary was invited to stay in context of all the subsequent problems that have now been disclosed in regards to abuse of children in residential schools. Her response is paraphrased by her granddaughter, Hilistis Pauline Waterfall: "The old people knew that one day, the outsiders would stay and outnumber the Heiltsuk. These outsiders would make laws that would diminish our way of life. This missionary's spiritual beliefs did not differ from ours. So, he was invited to stay – not to teach us about Christianity, but to teach us the new skills we would need in order to adapt to the changes that would greatly impact our future generations."

So the Heiltsuk have a tradition of adapting creatively to change, and welcoming people with specialized knowledge to contribute to their understanding of

their own world, and of the *waax-wais* as a whole. But for the most part, scientists, environmentalists, industry and government have conducted their innumerable studies of land and resources on the central coast of British Columbia while routinely overlooking the cultural values and knowledge held by the people who live there. There has been an almost ritual failure to recognize that decisions about natural resources – whether to allocate them for harvest, lock them up in a park, or otherwise exploit them – have profound and lasting consequences for people, especially indigenous people, whose relationship to their lands and waters literally defines them.

In the late 1990s, a new inquiry was begun on the central coast. The Heiltsuk Cultural Landscape Assessment is a community driven process to develop a comprehensive information base about Heiltsuk territory, and then to articulate a far-reaching vision of sustainable use and conservation of land and resources, based on Heiltsuk values.

The Heiltsuk Cultural Landscape Assessment was born in part out of the deficiencies of the conventional land use planning and regulatory tools of governments and industry, which fail to address the dual challenges of ecological conservation and economic development that the Heiltsuk constantly confront. Land use planning processes, such as provincial Land and Resource Management Plans (LRMPs), are divorced from the principles of community economic development, from the cultural values of First Nations peoples, and from traditional ecological knowledge. The Heiltsuk Cultural Landscape Assessment is based on an integration of all these things, along with mainstream science.

At first glance, the conservation values found within the Heiltsuk traditional territory seem obvious: the territory includes landscapes of world significance, with large areas of coastal temperate rain forest untouched by logging, and healthy populations of wildlife species such as deer, wolves, grizzly bear and mountain goat. However, this is an outsider's perspective of the area's conservation values, and does not tell the whole story.

From the Heiltsuk point of view, there are many natural features of the land that may not be rated as globally or even provincially significant, yet they are crucially important to the people who live in the region. Moreover, the Heiltsuk are not apt to view the landscape in terms such as "pristine" or "untouched", which excite the enthusiasm of outside conservationists. Instead, the conservation value of the land from the Heiltsuk perspective is centred on the wholeness and health of the land, both as a repository of natural diversity and as a cornucopia to support human society in a mutual and sustainable relationship. Rather than seeking to protect the land *from* human use, the Heiltsuk goal is to protect the land *for* human use – the kind of use that has sustained their ancestors for thousands of years.

Heiltsuk conservation goals tend to be more comprehensive than those of outsiders. As well, those goals are rooted in the understanding that future generations need to inherit the same level of natural abundance as the current generation. For example, a small stream supporting a run of 500 chum salmon might seem like an ordinary and unremarkable resource to government or industry planners. But from the Heiltsuk perspective, the same salmon run may be a crucial part of one or several household economies that has fed the family for countless generations. There may be stories and customs associated with a stream, even a Nameless Creek, that make it entirely unique. Every salmon stream, every bay where herring spawn, every stand of cedar trees – all of these are vital strands in the complex fabric of the Heiltsuk homeland, and vital sources of sustenance for Heiltsuk people. For example, there is evidence of more than 100 fish traps found in the territory's river systems. These

The conservation value of the land from the Heiltsuk perspective is centred on the wholeness and health of the land, both as a repository of natural diversity and as a cornucopia to support human society in a mutual and sustainable relationship

Heiltsuk Cultural Landscape Assessment information sharing meeting in Vancouver, January, 2001. Left to right: Robert Germyn, Chief Heiltsuk Councillor, William Gladstone, Heiltsuk Councillor, Cecil Reid, Heiltsuk Councillor, and Sandra Baan of International Forest Products.
DOUG HOPWOOD

Rather than fall victim to outside processes that are inherently bound to fail the Heiltsuk, the Heiltsuk have created their own process – the Heiltsuk Cultural Landscape Assessment.

are the clearest examples of traditional conservation practices. At high tide, salmon were caught in the rock traps that were strategically formed to utilize natural elements such as tidal action. Only what was needed for food was taken – often, the strongest and healthiest were left to go up the rivers to propagate. Yet, when these rock traps were discovered by outsiders, they were systemically dismantled for reasons only known to others. With every fish trap destroyed, another strand in the Heiltsuk's fabric was broken, and another source of knowledge was lost.

Through many decades of interaction with government and resource industries, and through countless frustrations and disappointments, the Heiltsuk have learned that if they are to be a voice for stewardship of their land and resources, they must deploy their own knowledge, hone their own expertise, gather and trust their own data, refine their tools for analysis, and equal if not better the analyses put forth by outsiders. It simply doesn't work for the Heiltsuk to present their concerns to government or industry or conservation groups jostling for ascendancy, and then stand on the sidelines waiting for their information to be incorporated into land use plans at the discretion of the triumphant outsider.

The Heiltsuk realize that access to high quality information and analysis about the land and resources is one of the keys to taking control of land use planning in their territory. Rather than fall victim to outside processes that are inherently bound to fail, the Heiltsuk have created their own process – the Heiltsuk Cultural Landscape Assessment.

The Heiltsuk Cultural Landscape Assessment grew out of conversations in Bella Bella that began between Ian Gill, president of Ecotrust Canada, and Edwin Newman Sr., chief treaty negotiator for the Heiltsuk people and a respected community leader. Gill's group had been working with the Haisla Nation for several years in territory that neighbours, and actually overlaps, Heiltsuk territory. Newman made it abundantly clear that the Heiltsuk were tired of being studied, and didn't want their territory turned into a park. "I don't like environmentalists," Newman told Gill. "You people always just want to stop things. My people need jobs." Gill told Newman that Ecotrust Canada was different, that it championed something called conservation-based development, that it was in fact looking for the intersection of economy and environment, rather than favouring one at the expense of the other. Newman's response didn't change much for a couple of years, and it wasn't just an expression of his personal bias. For the Heiltsuk, Ecotrust Canada had simply joined the choir of people from outside who drowned out what the Heiltsuk had to say.

Over time, however, it became clear that Ecotrust Canada had technical and analytical capacity that could help the Heiltsuk articulate their vision for the territory. So initially, Ecotrust Canada was invited to provide training and support in Geographic Information Systems to the Heiltsuk Treaty Office. In part this was because mapping and information management were identified as urgent areas for capacity building, but the early focus on assistance of a purely technical nature allowed time to build trust in the partnership between the Heiltsuk people and Ecotrust Canada. In order to be guided by the community in design and management of the project, the ability to communicate with community members is essential. Yet members of the community may regard communication with non-Heiltsuk workers as a waste of time, having seen many outsiders come and go with little evidence of long-term interest in the Heiltsuk community. The required level of trust can only be built in the context of a multi-year project. The Heiltsuk Cultural Landscape Assessment (HCLA)is just such a project. It was formally launched in December, 1998, with the signing of a protocol agreement between the Heiltsuk and Ecotrust Canada.

From the outset it was understood that it was essential to keep the project grounded in the community and to focus on building capacity and skills: "The Heiltsuk Treaty Office and Ecotrust Canada are committed to providing training and professional development opportunities for Heiltsuk people first and foremost, and will build this into all of our activities. Whenever possible, Heiltsuk professionals will be hired. If not, we will ensure that trainees work side-by-side with consultants." (From the protocol agreement between Ecotrust Canada and the Heiltsuk Treaty Office, December 1998).

Although external pressures – elections, resource development plans, funding shortfalls, LRMPs, environmental campaigns and the like – create a sense of urgency, the project has moved forward at a natural pace that allows for community consultation, and ensures that the community benefits directly through capacity building during the process, and not just with the final product.

After the protocol agreement between Ecotrust Canada and the Heiltsuk Treaty Office was signed, a methodology workshop was held in Bella Bella, bringing together local and external expertise to figure out how to actually do the HCLA. It was an important opportunity to introduce the project to the wider community, to have

the external scientists contribute feedback, to formulate a core working group of people and most importantly, to hear from the Heiltsuk community about basic guiding principles (see sidebar below) and priorities for the project.

That workshop led to the formation of the project's two main guiding bodies: an internal working group which includes a hereditary chief, youth, and elected council members; and an external advisory group made up of consultants from other First

Heiltsuk Cultural Landscape Assessment: Guiding Principles

This is a list of guiding principles, developed by the internal working group, with input from chiefs, elders and community members. These principles are written down to help guide us in our work, and to remind us of the values, laws, and philosophies which form the foundation for this project.

- We, the Heiltsuk, have been here since time immemorial and whatever we do must support the social, emotional, spiritual, physical and economic well being of the Heiltsuk for generations to come.

- We seek to understand and recognize the traditional roles of chiefs and others in managing and caring for our resources.

- We seek to incorporate the Heiltsuk traditional system of environmental knowledge.

- We acknowledge the importance of a unified strategy to protect and enhance aboriginal rights and title through good research, management, negotiations, practice of rights, and education.

- All activities in Heiltsuk territory will benefit the Heiltsuk people as a whole and not interfere with our aboriginal rights and title and our traditional reliance upon our land and resources.

- We acknowledge the importance of involving elders and encouraging our youth to participate in decisions regarding the management of our lands.

- The Heiltsuk are not separate from the natural environment and are in fact as much a part of this landscape, if not more so, than some of the very things that other people fight so hard to protect.

- Education begins with us. It is our responsibility to teach our children values that make us distinctly Heiltsuk.

Nations, foresters, ecologists, and social research scientists. The role of the internal working group is to ensure the project remains firmly grounded in the community and in Heiltsuk cultural values. Internal working group members meet regularly to set the direction of the project and provide a crucial link between project workers and the community.

One of the practical challenges of the project has been to develop effective processes of community consultation. People in First Nation communities are busy. Heiltsuk cultural life involves a rich schedule of work, social, and ceremonial events. No one has time to waste on poorly presented or repetitive information. Project workers are challenged to provide the right amount of detail, and to find the right balance between community consultation and independent initiative.

The external advisory group has less frequent contact with the project, but provides scientific and technical consultation to ensure that high standards of research methods and scientific analysis are maintained. Indeed, a thorough commitment to high research standards is an essential feature of the project. Given that the community is involved in treaty negotiations and, at various times, litigation about aboriginal rights and title, the results of the HCLA may be used to support negotiations or court pleadings, so it is essential all research be able to withstand detailed scientific and legal scrutiny.

Similarly, in the field of conservation science and resource management, initiatives such as the Scientific Panel for Sustainable Forest Practices in Clayoquot Sound illustrate that high quality scientific analysis carries a level of credibility and authority that is necessary when confronting the entrenched status quo of resource management.

The methodology of the Heiltsuk Cultural Landscape Assessment is, of necessity, innovative and adaptive, and this is in harmony with traditional oral ways of transmitting knowledge and wisdom. There is no textbook to consult, and the supply of practitioners experienced in this kind of research is limited. As a result, the HCLA team has devoted considerable energy to periodic evaluations of progress, and refining goals and methodologies.

Throughout the project, workers keep in mind that the final results must truly integrate traditional ecological knowledge with ecosystem science and enjoy wide support by different sectors of the Heiltsuk community; the project must use replicable methodologies and analysis, suitable for other communities on the coast; and the project must withstand legal and scientific scrutiny. The ultimate indication of success will be a functioning conservation-based development plan for Heiltsuk territory, one which contributes to economic and community well-being of the Heiltsuk, protects and honours Heiltsuk culture, and sustains the ecological wealth of the area.

The Heiltsuk Cultural Landscape Assessment represents a radical departure from traditional Western planning. For example, the approach to conservation that has been adopted by the B.C. government is a land-use planning system used widely in Canada and globally. This system calls for the setting aside of limited areas of land (and more recently, marine ecosystems) as parks, ecological reserves, or protected areas, in which resource harvesting is prohibited or severely curtailed. Outside these areas, the vast majority of the land or marine area is then made available for exploitation on an industrial scale. The forestry paradigm of "maximum sustained yield" tends to prevail on the non-protected areas. The land is thus artificially divided into either parks or the so-called working forest, both subject to strongly contrasting but equally rigid rules governing harvesting or human use activities. According to this reductionist and dualistic approach, selected areas are deemed "special" while most parts of the landscape are considered

The Heiltsuk Cultural Landscape Assessment represents a radical departure from traditional Western planning

ordinary and interchangeable. This approach is fundamentally contrary to the Heiltsuk aboriginal view in which the landscape is a seamless interconnected whole, and all areas are infused with a unique sacredness.

Protection of areas thought to have high ecological or recreational value has typically taken place without the knowledge or consent of the Heiltsuk, contrary to the consensus-building process that the Heiltsuk traditionally practiced. Because protection includes alienating First Nations from conducting traditional resource activities in parts of their traditional territory, it should come as no surprise that many First Nations, despite their commitment to conservation, have not supported the establishment of protected areas within their territories. The previous B.C. Ministry of Environment, Lands and Parks trumpeted the Hakai Recreation Area – encompassing more than 120,000 hectares of land and sea – as "the largest provincial marine park on the British Columbia coast." The Heiltsuk do not trumpet it at all. It is hard to get enthusiastic about a park that was created without Heiltsuk consent, devoting to the uses of non-Heiltsuk recreationists 200 times more areas than all the reserve lands the Heiltsuk were assigned a century or so ago.

The Hakai Recreation Area was designated with no understanding that the Heiltsuk viewed specific sites as traditional gathering places. For example, each spring the whole community moved to Goose Island where there is a long, sandy beach and abundant halibut fishing grounds. This was their annual sports day event, when friendly team sports took place along with competitive youth games that reinforced critical hunting and survival skills. This festivity marked the Heiltsuk New Year. With the winter supply of dried food running low, spring's arrival meant fresh seafood. The annual cycle of herring spawn provided the food base upon which halibut and other ground fish fed. In turn, these fish were readily caught and much appreciated.

In early 2001, some remedy appeared to be underway in respect of the Hakai. As an example of their increasing influence and authority, the Heiltsuk persuaded the provincial government to alter the designation of the area to Hakai Conservation Study Area and commit to working with the Heiltsuk in developing a land use designation that will respect Heiltsuk cultural and historical concerns.

It is also hard for the Heiltsuk to get enthusiastic about government planning processes for developing the region. Concurrent with the Cultural Landscape Assessment being undertaken by the Heiltsuk, the government has been conducting the Central Coast Land and Coastal Resource Management Plan (CCLCRMP), a land use planning process encompassing the Heiltsuk and other neighbouring First Nations territories. The CCLCRMP is designed as a round-table process, in which a wide range of stakeholders are asked to work towards a consensus on the location of protected areas, and the establishment of broad resource management goals for the region.

From the Heiltsuk point of view, the CCLCRMP process is critically flawed, because it fails to acknowledge aboriginal title. The province claims that land use designations arising from the CCLCRMP will be "without prejudice" to future land claim settlements or treaties, but it is clear that such designations will create expectations among third party groups, such as forest companies, tourism businesses, and the recreational public, that will put political if not legal constraints on the negotiation of land claim settlements. Moreover, the CCLCRMP process has the effect of elevating such third party interests to the status of decision-making partners in the long-term future of First Nations territories. This includes individuals who do not live in the region, and whose only connection is that they hold commercial resource tenures awarded by the provincial government. Such people may have been involved in the area for just a few years.

Consider, for example, the political influence wielded by investors and operators in the various "dive fisheries" that have recently developed on the coast. On the north coast, an area that includes Heiltsuk territory, there has been a staggering increase in the value of the dive fishery in the past two decades. The value of catches of four main species – geoduck, abalone, red sea urchin and sea cucumber – rose from $1.3-million in 1984 to $33-million by 1995. According to Kelly Brown, then senior treaty negotiator for the Heiltsuk Nation, the fate of abalone is a classic example of resource depletion in the region. At an information sharing session on the HCLA in January, 2001, Brown said:

"I'm going to show you one example of a resource that's very close to extinction from our territory. It's the abalone. And that's because of the commercial fishing industry for that resource. The Heiltsuk people and the way they harvested that particular resource never, ever dove for that particular resource. As you know, the abalone commercial fishery is a diving fishery and they dive for the abalone. The Heiltsuk people never harvested the abalone below the low watermark. There's a reason for that. Below the low watermark was the bank, as far as our territory was concerned. And we always knew that that resource would always come back if we didn't dive for that resource. And we believe that as Heiltsuk people, that if that resource was available to us it was on the beaches during low tide. The Heiltsuk people have always been conservationists since time immemorial. We never, as Heiltsuk people, over-harvested our resources in our lifetime. It's only been over the past 100 years that any one resource has ever disappeared to almost extinction from our territory."

None of the government processes to date have come close to enabling the Heiltsuk to articulate a vision of the conservation economy in their territory

Due to stock depletion because of the commercial fishery, the abalone fishery was closed after 1990, and Heiltsuk people were denied access to a favourite food their ancestors had conserved and enjoyed for millennia. Yet at a process like the CCLCRMP, "stakeholder" status is afforded to resource harvesters – abalone fishermen among them – who have a demonstrated stake in resource extraction, but have shown minimal restraint in view of pressures on the stock, and whose activity depletes food the Heiltsuk have traditionally relied upon.

Back in Chief Bob Anderson's day, outside exploitation of fisheries was already an issue: "We would be very glad if you would help us in regard to our fishing licences... We think that the money which has been received for all these fishing licences in the past should have been, and should be paid over to us, all the fishing privileges rightly belong to us Indians. The place is ours."

On the land, the provincial planning system proposes in theory that there should be a spectrum of land use intensities. Protection in parks or other reserves is one path. Designation of Special Management Zones (SMZs) is another. The notion of SMZs was introduced in the Vancouver Island Land Use Plan and was meant to create a middle ground between the extremes of no harvesting and intensive industrial use. However, the concept of SMZs was effectively sabotaged by a cabinet directive that within SMZs, levels of logging could not be reduced by more than 10 per cent relative to what would occur in the absence of the SMZ designation. As a result, SMZs provide little opportunity to explore any real alternative to the dominant paradigm, derived from an agricultural model, in which forests are exploited at levels close to their maximum theoretical production. Hence, the concept of ecosystem management – the notion of focusing first on ecosystem integrity and only secondly on extraction and yield – remains elusive in B.C. One emerging example – although tiny in relation to the dominant industrial model of forestry in B.C. – is that of Iisaak Forest Resources Ltd., a joint venture between the Nuu-chah-nulth First Nation of Vancouver Island and Weyerhaeuser Company Ltd. Iisaak's operations are designed to be consistent with the Clayoquot Sound Scientific Panel recommendations, which put ecosystem integrity ahead of harvest volumes. A similar paradigm underlies the Heiltsuk Cultural Landscape Assessment.

As the HCLA moves from an information-gathering phase to concrete analysis, planning and action, a major challenge is to broaden the concepts of land use designation beyond the limited palette of the provincial land use planning system. There will be a need for land use designations that incorporate traditional Heiltsuk concepts, while dealing effectively with the challenges of modern harvesting and management technologies. Certainly, none of the government processes to date have come close to enabling the Heiltsuk to articulate a vision of the conservation economy in their territory.

One problem is poor information. The HCLA's partners are dedicated to sound methodology and high research standards, but are constrained by available data. Much of the forest inventory data available from government and industry is of poor quality and has major gaps and inconsistencies. For example, the Ministry of Forests bases its analyses of timber supply, and in turn determines the Allowable Annual Cut for major tenures in the territory, on weak and obsolete information about the extent, quality, and growth rates of harvestable timber. Given the large area of land in the territory, it would be far beyond the financial resources of the HCLA to collect new data for the whole territory. The HCLA approach is to make the best of existing information, while recognizing its uncertainties and limitations.

Over-commitment and declining yields of key resources such as timber and salmon creates a resource squeeze, such that government agencies and non-native resource users often have a defensive attitude, suspicious of or overtly hostile to any proposed change. This atmosphere of scarcity, combined with the failure of governments and industry to acknowledge Heiltsuk rights and jurisdiction, means that the planning aspect of the HCLA is conducted against a backdrop of political and legal struggles over jurisdiction and resource allocation that threaten to obscure the long-term goals of the HCLA. At the same time, the globally significant conservation values of Heiltsuk territory have attracted the involvement of national and international conservation groups and created a tense, high stakes atmosphere around conservation issues in the territory. In addition, the Heiltsuk community faces short-term pressures of many kinds. For example, threats to salmon habitat and culturally modified trees from numerous logging operations in the territory tend to draw scarce

Companies like Iisaak Forest Resources are paving the way for the future of sustainable resource extraction. Here, an Iisaak forester selectively chooses the best timber for harvesting.
CINDY HAZENBOOM

resources of personnel and funding into "fighting brush fires," as in the case of Nameless Creek. These are resources that might ultimately be better used in the more comprehensive and long-term approach of the HCLA.

The HCLA incorporates products of diverse kinds: capacity building, data collection, analysis, and development of a community-based vision and strategy. These products are in three broad areas: culture, ecological and management science, and conservation-based development. The HCLA is based on a comprehensive research model (see sidebar opposite page) that seeks a synergistic integration of research in these diverse fields.

The Heiltsuk Traditional Use Study (TUS), coordinated by the Heiltsuk Cultural Education Centre in Bella Bella is a cornerstone of the HCLA, because it provides a clear documented record of the rich array of ecological knowledge and traditional uses that is needed to integrate Heiltsuk cultural values and participation into resource planning and analysis.

With respect to conservation planning, the HCLA aims to merge the site-specific ecological knowledge held by the community with science-based information such as ecosystem classification, stream inventories and wildlife habitat modelling. One of the strengths of the science-based approach is that resource inventories and analysis generally cover the entire territory with a single consistent methodology. For example, biologists working for the previous Ministry of Environment, Lands and Parks have created habitat models for several wildlife species including black-tailed deer, mountain goats, and grizzly bear. Such models are based on data such as climate, vegetation, slope, and aspect of the land. These data in turn are derived largely from topographic maps, air photos, and satellite images. The degree to which these data are verified by on the ground surveys varies, but is almost never enough to account for small-scale local ecological factors that can affect wildlife habitat, such as the presence of salt licks that attract mountain goats. Traditional ecological knowledge (TEK), collected and organized through the traditional use study, can often provide this kind of missing detail. On the other hand, TEK data may lack the spatial completeness and consistency of the science-based approach, simply because individual interviewees may present their information in different ways, or some traditional knowledge may have been lost over time.

According to traditional use researcher Terry Tobias: "Land use and occupancy mapping employs the rules of social science, which studies society and social relationships. The practice of it is social in nature because one person is asking another for information, and it is science because the questions are being asked in a systematic manner, according to Western scientific rules of gathering and verifying knowledge." Ideally, the science-based and traditional approaches complement and enhance each other.

Another important cultural component of the HCLA is an archaeological potential model that provides a broad-scale coarse-filter method for predicting the occurrence of culturally modified trees and aboriginally logged areas, based on forest cover data,

Heiltsuk stream inventory crew, seen here, were able to assess damage done by logging companies to fish habitat in their territory by using a combination of local traditional knowledge and rigorous modern scientific survey methods.
MIKE JACOBS

While many First Nations have been involved in Traditional Use Studies, many of these studies do not meet the needs of First Nations in establishing their rights and titles. An effective approach to collecting traditional use data is "comprehensive research," a strategy that links a number of key research products together to produce data which prove that mapped land use and occupancy information represents living cultural systems.

In contrast to comprehensive research, the "museum approach" is industry and government's typical interpretation of mapped First Nation cultural features, as isolated remnants of a dead or dying tradition, instead of elements of living cultural systems.

The components of comprehensive research fall into two categories. On the "indigenous side" are projects such as studies of traditional harvesting and ecological knowledge, indigenous place names, genealogy, social customs, and maps of harvesting sites and cultural sites. These studies depend on information that can only be acquired from living First Nations people. In the past, provincial agencies have not regarded information of this kind as worthy of consideration in management decisions. On the "Western management" side are projects such as natural resource inventories and analysis, fish and wildlife studies, and economic studies of forestry, tourism, etc.

Indigenous and Western management research, when combined, provide explanations and context to help understand peoples' relationships to the First Nations' territories and resources. And this includes all people and interests: First Nations, governments, and third parties. Of particular interest to First Nations, of course, is the enhancement of title and rights, but beyond this, the products of comprehensive research can be synthesized for use in an integrated resource management plan to protect First Nations' interests while accommodating others' interests as much as possible.

Most First Nations lack sufficient funding and capacity to complete a full suite of comprehensive research studies within the short time frames mandated by outside pressures and processes. However, there is a research model emerging that is available to any community wanting comprehensive indigenous side research, that is based on seven overarching principles:

- The community's political commitment to comprehensive research is based on the First Nation's vision for itself, not on the existence or outcome of any particular framework agreement or process.

- Research undertaken by communities belonging to the same nation adopts similar methodologies and the same high standards.

- Each research component explains or demonstrates some aspect of a nation's relationship to its territory.

- Each research component is done according to best practices.

- Each research component builds on the strengths of previous and concurrent research.

- Channels between each research component and all other concurrent research being done by the nation stay wide open.

- The nation's "culture of research" is encouraged at every opportunity.

Many First Nations have obtained significant research funds over the past few decades. Unfortunately, funding that comes without adequate training and "how-to" manuals is often spent on poor quality research. Some communities have done three mapping projects over the years – each covering the same area and data – but decided not to use the maps in negotiations because of poor quality. Elders often say, "We've been studied to death." If all the funds and community effort had been spent on best practices research with a comprehensive strategy, the nation could have acquired a solid research package by now.

Regarding the time frame, whether it takes three years or ten years, the need for good research is inescapable. Enhancing title and rights requires it, management of land and resources requires it, and self-government requires it. Even a single quality piece of research in hand can move the yardsticks forward in concrete ways. Two or three complementary pieces of research can be very effective in a negotiation. When it's quality work, every bit strengthens the First Nation's position.

topography, distance from water, and proximity to known archaeological sites. Through the leadership of the Heiltsuk Cultural Education Centre, this tool will help in the struggle to protect these valuable artifacts from the impacts of logging, and can help inform community members of the extent of traditional uses.

Since 1997, Ecotrust Canada has worked with Heiltsuk Treaty Office staff in Bella Bella on a training program in GIS and associated skills such as interpretation of forest inventory data. The tangible result of this work is that the Heiltsuk GIS office now has the capacity to handle all the GIS needs of the community's traditional use study, and produces many of the maps and analyses required by the treaty office.

One of the initial accomplishments of the HCLA has been to collect existing map layers from government and organize them into a single comprehensive GIS database. This data enables project workers to address questions about resource issues in the territory, and to create maps that help to clarify these issues for community members. This GIS database includes information on forest cover, tenures, ecological classifications, and a variety of maps prepared for the LRMP, such as the locations

of tourism facilities or areas identified as high priority for grizzly bear conservation.

At the outset, a complete inventory was conducted of all relevant data held by the Heiltsuk Treaty Office and the Heiltsuk Tribal Council, both in digital and paper formats. After a data library and catalogue was created it was possible to do a preliminary data gap analysis, which revealed a serious lack of information with regard to streams and fish habitat. This led to the initiation of a multi-year stream inventory study that has been one of the most important aspects of the project to date.

The Heiltsuk stream inventory project, supported in part by the David Suzuki Foundation, is a good example of combining the collection of much-needed data with skills development. Under the direction of the fisheries co-management office and Mike Jacobs, a Heiltsuk crew surveyed 100 streams in Heiltsuk territory during the 2000 field season. The survey covered about 50 kilometres of streams in total. A crew of four people, plus a boat skipper, conducted inventories of up to seven salmonid species, fish habitat assessments, fry trapping and identification, surveyed fish trap locations, and recorded evidence of historical logging. In keeping with the principle of high quality research, a total of 10 Heiltsuk workers completed training and achieved certification to provincial Resources Inventory Committee standards, so the data they gathered can be viewed as credible and reliable by all users. In addition, they were trained in safety and wilderness first aid, orienteering, field note keeping and general salmonid biology.

The capacity-building component of the HCLA is not limited to training at a technical level. For example, in June of 2000, two Heiltsuk Nation staff visited Powell River to study how the Sliammon First Nation deals with the complex challenges of responding to the various logging and land use plans it receives for comments, a system known as the referrals process. The result was a constructive exchange of ideas and methods for organizing information systems, setting priorities,

Many members of the Heiltsuk Nation are participating in the Heiltsuk Cultural Landscape Assessment, gaining first hand knowledge about the land and their territory. Caroline Hall, Heiltsuk GIS technician. KIRA GERWING

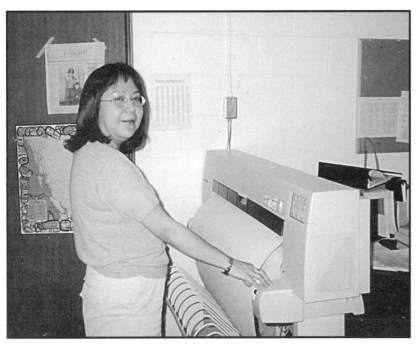

Tommy Humchitt working on a non-timber forest product study of pine mushrooms in Heiltsuk Traditional Territory.
SIGNY FREDERICKSON

and funding the referrals department. In addition, a professional forester on contract to the HCLA project has worked part-time with the Heiltsuk Forestry Coordinator in conducting site visits and formulating responses to forest development plans.

Certification of forestry operations and forest products is one of the keys to moving from status quo to sustainable forest practices in the territory. To help community members understand the issues of certification, the HCLA project hosted an information workshop on the Forest Stewardship Council certification process in Bella Bella. And in order to see first-hand an example of an FSC-certified, First Nations owned and operated, conservation-based forest products enterprise, a delegation of Heiltsuk band members visited Iisaak Forest Resources' Clayoquot Sound operations in February 2001.

One of the objectives of the HCLA is to explore economic development opportunities that are compatible with maintaining natural capital. In other forested regions, harvesting of non-timber forest products (NTFPs) such as mushrooms, floral greens, and herbal or medicinal plants, has provided a viable alternative to logging for forest-based employment, but little is known about the potential for NTFPs in the Heiltsuk territory. A comprehensive study to fill in the knowledge gaps was begun in August 2000. An inter-disciplinary team is studying the distribution of NTFP resources in the territory and assessing the potential for economic development. The NTFP study is a good example of the need to integrate cultural knowledge with scientific studies and economic development initiatives, because many plants that have commercial potential may be important resources in traditional Heiltsuk culture. Also, they may be regarded as sacred or their harvest may be subject to particular rules or customs. Attempts to commercialize these resources without careful consideration of the cultural

Certification of forestry operations and forest products is one of the keys to moving from status quo to sustainable forest practices in the territory

factors could interfere with traditional non-commercial uses, or might be contrary to traditional teachings. And, information about traditional uses of plants may be proprietary knowledge that should not be used commercially without providing compensation. For these reasons, the NTFP study team was led by a professional ethnobotanist, was conducted in close coordination with the Heiltsuk Cultural Education Centre, and included consultation with Heiltsuk elders on matters of cultural sensitivity.

Although much of Heiltsuk traditional territory has not been logged, some watersheds have been heavily impacted by industrial forestry that has damaged salmon habitat in the streams, and caused loss of wildlife habitat associated with old growth forests. Analysis will be undertaken to set priorities for watershed restoration. As in other areas of the HCLA, the criteria for setting such priorities will integrate scientific and cultural information. Sources of biophysical data include stream surveys (size of fish runs, quality of fish habitat, degree of impact from logging), forest inventories (logging history, road density, and degree of natural recovery), wildlife habitat models, and local knowledge. Cultural data such as location of traditional fishing sites and the presence of fish traps or other archaeological features helps to clarify the cultural context of the biophysical resources. Part of the restoration strategy will also be to identify opportunities for Heiltsuk people to become involved in restoration work.

A critical aim of the HCLA is to move beyond information gathering and into targeted analysis. One example is the Heiltsuk Total Cut Database, a study that documented the volumes, species, grades, and values of timber harvested in the territory, and the stumpage paid to government. The preliminary finding is that the 1999 Canadian dollar value of all timber cut in Heiltsuk territory to date is roughly

Such findings provide a powerful negotiating tool for the Heiltsuk in treaty or other negotiations with government and industry

$2 billion. Of this huge sum, the Heiltsuk have received no royalties or other compensation, and the indirect benefit has been limited to a small number of seasonal logging jobs that have been available to Heiltsuk workers on a sporadic basis. Clearly, such findings provide a powerful negotiating tool for the Heiltsuk in treaty or other negotiations with government and industry, as well as critical information to include in market-based campaigns intended to promote more equitable distribution of the benefits of resource use in First Nations territories.

A priority for the Cultural Landscape Assessment has been to come to grips with forestry issues in Heiltsuk territory, by collecting inventory data, analyzing trends, and developing practical alternatives to the current pattern of destructive resource depletion.

Heiltsuk traditional territory comprises 1.7 million hectares of land, of which approximately one-third is forested. Virtually all of the commercially valuable forest in the territory outside of protected areas is under some form of tenure that provides harvesting rights to logging companies.

To understand what is happening with the forest resources of Heiltsuk territory, it is necessary to look beyond the boundaries of the territory, because the government of B.C. and the forest companies historically have treated the territory as just one part of several larger units of forest land. Under the Forest Act, which governs forest tenures and allowable cuts in B.C., a separate Allowable Annual Cut (AAC) is set for each Timber Supply Area (TSA) or Tree Farm Licence (TFL). However, these are large units of land and there is no regulation to ensure that the cut is distributed evenly throughout the TSA or TFL. On the contrary, in most cases logging has been highly concentrated in the areas with the most valuable timber and easiest access.

Seventy-one percent of the Heiltsuk territory's land area lies within the mid-coast TSA, but some of the most productive and easily accessible forest land

in the TSA is located outside Heiltsuk territory, in the large river valleys in the south and eastern portion of the TSA. Much of the past logging in the mid-coast TSA was concentrated in the valuable old-growth Douglas-fir stands of the Bella Coola Valley, South Bentinck Arm, Owikeno Lake, Rivers Inlet, Boswell Inlet and Smith Inlet. These resources have now been depleted, and in order to maintain the level of cut, the logging companies are finding it necessary to concentrate the cut in new areas, mostly within Heiltsuk traditional territory. As a result, the current rate of cut within the territory is much higher than the long-term sustainable rate.

Map 5.1 on page 127 illustrates past and future logging in the Heiltsuk Traditional Territory. The bright red shows areas slated for logging within the next five years (based on data available as of 1998). The B.C. Ministry of Forests sets the Allowable Annual Cut for the TSA as a whole, but allows

companies to concentrate their logging in the most valuable stands. Past logging has depleted the rich valley-bottom forests on the southeastern extent of the TSA, outside the Heiltsuk territory. Because these areas are now depleted, to maintain their Annual Allowable Cut, logging companies are now cutting in the forests of the Heiltsuk traditional territory at a rate that far exceeds the capacity for re-growth.

The detrimental impacts of such concentrated cutting are illustrated at Nameless Creek on the Don Peninsula in Heiltsuk Territory, where the five-year logging plan calls for clearcutting 15 per cent of the watershed area in two years. By contrast, the Scientific Panel for Sustainable Forest Practices in Clayoquot Sound (1995) recommended that the rate of cut in watersheds over 500 hectares should not exceed five per cent in any five-year period. A rate of cut of 15.3 per cent in two years is likely to be very detrimental to salmon habitat in the Nameless Creek watershed. Through a combined approach of mapping and analysis the HCLA has revealed the problem of concentration of harvest in Heiltsuk territory, and how it is leading to unsound logging practices that threaten environmental qualities and infringe on Heiltsuk aboriginal rights.

The concentration of cut is dire enough purely in terms of the hectares logged every year. But in the past few years the Heiltsuk have noticed an even more alarming trend. The areas targeted for logging in recent years are increasingly likely to be stands of large old-growth cedar.

The most common type of forest in Heiltsuk territory consists of a mix of western hemlock and amabilis fir, known in forestry jargon

As work on the Heiltsuk Cultural Landscape Assessment progresses, so does industrial logging in Heiltsuk Traditional Territory, such as that pictured on Yeo Island. DAVE NUNUK

These resources have now been depleted, and in order to maintain the level of cut, the logging companies are finding it necessary to concentrate the cut in new areas

as "hembal." The second most common type is forest of primarily western red cedar. Cedar is a much higher-value timber type than hembal; in fact, while cedar stands can be very profitable to log, many of the hembal stands cannot be logged at a profit under common market conditions. As a result, logging companies are resorting to the age-old practice of "high-grading", cutting the highest value stands and leaving the rest. The phenomenon of over-cutting cedar isn't just a problem in Heiltsuk territory. "We have been logging more cedar than is in the (forest) profile and that is a reflection of the economics," said Rick Jeffrey, president of the British Columbia Truck Loggers Association. Jeffrey said companies target cedar in the face of declining prices for lower-valued species like hemlock. Thus does the global market for wood have a direct and dramatic effect on the future prospects of the Heiltsuk people.

The concern is that if this trend continues, the result will be a forest of primarily hemlock and balsam, and little or no harvestable old-growth cedar will remain. Old-growth cedar is an essential resource for many Heiltsuk traditional uses, so depletion of the cedar resource would make these difficult to practice. Cedar is also more valuable than hemlock or balsam in the forest products market, so depletion of the cedar resource limits the opportunities for the Heiltsuk people to participate in the forest sector of the economy. As part of the Heiltsuk Cultural Landscape Assessment, staff at Ecotrust Canada undertook research to reveal the extent and implications of the cedar over-cut.

Two main sources of data were used in the analysis. Estimates of the volume harvested are taken from the Heiltsuk Total Cut Database, and estimates of the volume of old-growth timber available to log in the mid-coast TSA portion of the Heiltsuk traditional territory were derived from Ministry of Forests forest inventory files.

According to the methodology used by the Ministry of Forests to define the Timber Harvesting Land Base (THLB) in the most recent Timber Supply Review process, the estimated total volume of cedar on the THLB in the portion of the mid-coast TSA that lies within the Heiltsuk Traditional Territory, is 11,033,356 m^3 (cubic metres), which constitutes 23 per cent of the total timber volume (all species) calculated by the same methodology (the Timber Harvesting Land Base is the area of land that the Ministry of Forests assumes will be available to log, for the purpose of estimating future timber supply and setting the AAC).

To address the issue of a possible cedar over-cut, it was necessary to know the volume of timber harvested from the Heiltsuk territory each year, and what portion of that was cedar. This analysis indicates that a disproportionate harvesting of cedar is occurring in the Heiltsuk Territory portion of the TSA, with the 1999 harvest being 60 % cedar, even though cedar is only 23 % of the available forest inventory (see Figure 1).

This startling result raised a simple question – how long will it last? A model was developed to examine, in a preliminary way, the implications of this harvest pattern for the long-term availability of harvestable old-growth cedar. The year 1997 was chosen as the starting point, with 11,033,356 m^3 of cedar inventory as of 1996. For 1997, 1998, and 1999, the estimated actual harvest volumes (182,579 m^3, 164,759 m^3, and 294,140 m^3 respectively) were

Figure 1

YEAR	CEDAR CUT	CEDAR ON THLB
1989	27	23
1990	29	23
1991	22	23
1992	34	23
1993	30	23
1994	26	23
1995	27	23
1996	33	23
1997	33	23
1998	49	23
1999	59	23

subtracted, leaving 10,391,878 m³ as of 2000. For the subsequent period, three future harvest scenarios were tested. The future annual cedar harvest was tested at:

- the lowest level of any year in the period 1995 through 1999 (164,759 m³ in 1998);
- the average level for the period 1995 through 1999 (202,362 m³);
- the highest level of any year in the period 1995 through 1999 (294,140 m³ in 1999).

The results of this analysis indicate that:
- at a harvest rate of 164,759 m³/year (5-year low) all old-growth cedar on the THLB will be gone in 2063;
- at a harvest rate of 202,362 m³/year (5-year average) all old-growth cedar on the THLB will be gone in 2051;
- at a harvest rate of 294,140 m³/year (5-year high) all old-growth cedar on the THLB will be gone in 2035.

At current logging rates, the operable old-growth cedar could be gone in as little as 35 to 60 years, leaving a gap of several decades before any second-growth cedar becomes harvestable at about 80 years of age. However, 80-year-old second-growth cedar is not suitable for traditional uses such as canoes, or for market products that require tight grain clear wood, such as cedar roof shakes. Those uses require trees several hundred years old.

Cedar is an essential resource for a wide range of traditional uses such as buildings, canoes, bentwood boxes, and totem poles. Throughout Heiltsuk territory, ancient cedar trees are found with test holes chopped in them. These trees were not taken due to imperfections such as decay pockets. Such trees are found up to several kilometres from the ocean, providing striking proof that it has always been a challenge to find the right trees for the very demanding requirements of certain traditional uses. The contrast between traditional Heiltsuk tree-harvesting methods and industrial logging could hardly be more vivid. Traditionally,

Heiltsuk artist Ian Reid painting a carved house post to be used in the construction of a traditional Big House.
SETH ZUCKERMAN

the Heiltsuk concept of logging was to beachcomb for blow-down trees. A living tree was not used unless its dimensions met the criteria for building a canoe, long house or other specific use. If a tree had to be cut down, a song was sung to empathize with the pain it was enduring.

The HCLA forestry analysis has revealed two alarming trends in Heiltsuk traditional territory: the concentration of logging in the territory due to past over-cutting elsewhere, and the cutting of cedar far in excess of its proportion in the forest profile. Either of these trends would be damaging enough, but taken together, they mean that Heiltsuk territory is rapidly being stripped of the forest resources the Heiltsuk will need to build an economically secure and culturally rich future.

The Heiltsuk understand that a vibrant future must be based on a mix of preserving tradition and embracing the new. For this reason, over-cutting in

Heiltsuk youth gather around a culturally modified ancient cedar tree on Yeo Island in the Heiltsuk Traditional Territory. The hole chopped in the tree decades ago was used to determine if the tree was sound enough for a specific use such as making a canoe.
DOUG HOPWOOD

unemployment (roughly 70 to 80 per cent). These difficulties – typical of many coastal First Nations communities – are aggravated by geographic isolation and transportation obstacles. With the recent job losses in the fishing industry Heiltsuk people are looking to the forest as a possible source of economic development, and are determined to prevent "timber-mining" practices from causing a repeat of the tragic decline of the salmon fishery.

Although this analysis paints a bleak picture, it provides a necessary basis in planning for positive change. For example, simulations of future timber supply conducted by the Ministry of Forests and forest companies indicate that harvest volumes in Heiltsuk territory are likely to decline by at least five per cent per decade for the next 50 years. The projected decline would be much worse if the concentration of logging in the territory or the high-grading of cedar were taken into account. In order to investigate these concerns and develop estimates of sustainable timber harvest levels for the Heiltsuk territory the Heiltsuk Nation intends to undertake its own detailed timber supply analysis in collaboration with Ecotrust Canada.

It is clear that there is little point to the Heiltsuk trying to increase their prosperity simply by seeking a larger share of the logging jobs in their territory, since the number of such jobs is likely to be continually shrinking for many decades to come. There is little value in a forest management strategy that focuses on logging large volumes of timber to be processed outside the region, because more of the employment and profitability of the forest sector is in the manufacturing phase than in the initial logging.

High unemployment, combined with the failure of the provincial government to recognize aboriginal rights and title, has left many coastal First Nations feeling disempowered, despite landmark legal rulings in their favour, such as the decision in *Delgamuukw*. In such an environment, it is easy for forest companies to use the offer of logging jobs as an inducement for First Nations to sanction unsustainable logging in their territories.

general – compounded by the high-grading of cedar in particular – is doubly disturbing. The elevated rate of cedar logging in Heiltsuk territory – targeting the very stands most likely to contain good trees for traditional uses – can only increase the scarcity of such trees and further threaten the cultural future of the Heiltsuk people. Equally distressing, the current rates of cedar logging seriously jeopardize the opportunities for the Heiltsuk to build a secure economic future in the forest products sector.

As a result of rapid economic changes on the central coast, especially the decline of the salmon fishery and the centralization of fish processing, the Heiltsuk community of Bella Bella has high

To break out of this trap, the Heiltsuk must acquire control of their own forest tenures, giving them the power to plan for sustainable rates of harvest and to log using methods that do not damage salmon streams and other forest resources. Most of the timber in Heiltsuk territory is allocated to three large forest companies under two Tree Farm Licenses and two Forest Licenses. Tree Farm Licenses are called area-based tenures because the licensee is allocated a defined area of land where they enjoy a nearly exclusive right to log. Forest Licenses are known as volume-based tenures, because the license provides the right to cut a volume of timber each year without specifying a particular area of land from where the timber is to come. The term of a Tree Farm License is 25 years, but the tenure is in effect perpetual, due to the "evergreen clause" under which the provincial government must, by law, offer the licensee a replacement tenure on the fifth anniversary of the date the license was issued. A Forest License typically has a 15-year term with an evergreen clause for replacement on the fifth anniversary.

For more than 25 years, the Heiltsuk Tribal Council has been actively seeking a forest tenure in Heiltsuk territory, but with no success. Recently, the Ministry of Forests has indicated that a forest tenure may be made available to the Heiltsuk, but that it would be short term (3 to 7 years), temporary (no evergreen clause) and volume-based (no defined land area). A tenure of this form would provide no assurance of a sustainable long-term timber supply. Because there is no exclusive right to cut from a clearly defined land base, there is almost no opportunity to limit the rate of cut to stay within the long-term productive capacity of the land, or to plan the harvest in an integrated fashion to protect non-timber values on the forest landscape. In other words, the tenure available to the Heiltsuk, in their own traditional territory, would be inferior in every significant respect to the tenures held by major logging companies. Far from empowering the Heiltsuk to participate constructively in the forest sector, such a tenure would put the Heiltsuk at the back of a long line of interests vying for the right to log the rapidly dwindling timber resources of the territory.

Economic development based on natural resources is needed; however, conventional notions of economic development are not often directly applicable in First Nations communities such as Bella Bella, where traditional harvesting activities such as fishing and gathering seaweed are important elements of the local economy. Many families still derive a significant portion of their diet and other needs from the land. Economic development strategies must be compatible with the complex mix of wage employment, small businesses, and land and marine-based subsistence harvesting that constitute the economy of such communities. Wage employment and opportunities to operate small business are needed, but must be structured in ways that do not prevent participation in traditional activities.

In response to the largest campaign of civil disobedience in Canadian history, protesting destructive logging practices in Clayoquot Sound on Vancouver Island, the government of British Columbia appointed a panel of respected scientists to recommend forest practices for the Sound that would be the "best in the world." The Clayoquot Science Panel recommended sweeping changes not only to on-the-ground logging practices, but equally to the planning system used to develop logging plans. The similarities between Clayoquot Sound and the central coast are striking – the rugged terrain and maritime climate, the high conservation values of salmon streams and extensive old-growth forests, the presence of First Nations communities that maintain an intimate connection to the land and sea. Clearly, the recommendations of the Scientific

It is clear that there is little point to the Heiltsuk trying to increase their prosperity simply by seeking a larger share of the logging jobs in their territory, since the number of such jobs is likely to be continually shrinking for many decades to come

Panel for Sustainable Forest Practices in Clayoquot Sound would be widely applicable in the central coast with relatively minor changes to account for regional differences in ecological, economic or social conditions. Yet ironically, practices on the central coast have gone in the opposite direction under the industry-mandated drive to "streamline" the Forest Practices Code.

By clarifying what has gone seriously wrong with the *status quo* approach to forestry, the Heiltsuk Cultural Landscape Assessment is helping to define an alternative strategy designed to meet Heiltsuk needs for economic development and conservation of natural ecosystems. The essence of such a strategy would be to log less volume and add more value to it by processing locally – anything from log sorting, through saw-milling, and all the way up to producing very high-value items such as carvings or traditional buildings.

Oolichan fish being strung together on a cedar strip in preparation for drying. First Nations traditionally understood a reciprocal relationship with the land and sea, working to protect the environment, and being clothed, sheltered and fed in return. GARY FIEGEHEN

Another important opportunity to add value is by seeking Forest Stewardship Council certification for timber and products from Heiltsuk territory. The HCLA is providing information and support for the Heiltsuk Nation and individuals in understanding certification issues. It has also helped to alert the community to the urgent need for reforms to forest practices on Heiltsuk territory – lest the community inherit a forest bereft of cedar.

The HCLA is designed to be a multi-purpose planning tool, built by the Heiltsuk to be used by the Heiltsuk. Just as inputs to the process are a blend of cultural data, conservation science, and economic development planning, the outputs of the HCLA products are valuable in these same areas.

In part, the impetus to begin the project came from the needs of the Heiltsuk Treaty Office. As treaty negotiations with the Federal and Provincial governments got under way in the early 1990s, it became clear that the treaty office urgently needed its own information base and capacity for mapping and analysis. It was thought that in the long run, the treaty office would need to produce nothing less than a comprehensive long-term vision for sustaining the prosperity of the Heiltsuk people and the ecosystems of the Heiltsuk lands.

While produced under the auspices of the treaty office, the HCLA is needed regardless of the outcome of the treaty process. If a treaty is reached, both the capacity built through the HCLA and the information and analysis products themselves will be valuable as the Heiltsuk assume more roles as resource managers and decision-makers. Moreover, a treaty will not provide final and certain resolution of the complex land use issues in Heiltsuk territory, nor will it eliminate all third party interests.

Unfortunately, no First Nation in B.C. can afford to have full confidence in the treaty process as the means to reconciliation of land and resource issues. Throughout B.C., First Nations are increasingly frustrated and discouraged as government offers fall far short of the level of jurisdiction and access to resources that First Nations need to create lasting prosperity. In the event that no treaty settlement is reached, the Heiltsuk will have even greater need of the HCLA as they continue to struggle for cultural survival, economic independence, and stewardship of the land, through whatever process is open to them. This could include legal actions to seek verification of specific aboriginal rights.

In any event, the Heiltsuk are reclaiming their responsibility and authority as stewards of their land and resources. They will be increasingly proactive in all matters relating to their economic and cultural future and to stewardship of the land. The HCLA will provide baseline data documenting the current condition of the land and resources. This data will allow monitoring of change within the territory through periodic evaluation of specific indicators, such as the extent of old-growth forests or the condition of salmon streams. The HCLA will help in identifying opportunities for economic development, including forests suitable for supporting community-based forestry.

The HCLA will serve as a tool for cultural education and rediscovery, primarily through the Traditional Use Study (TUS). This study will provide a comprehensive database of a wide range of traditional activities conducted on the land. Information of this kind may be used in conjunction with the Qqs ("Eyes") Project, in which several rustic cabins have been built at significant locations around the territory, and are available for community members to use for traditional land-based activities such as fishing, crabbing, seaweed collecting, family retreats, or camps for youth programs. A potential synergy exists between the cabins and the TUS data. The cabins make it feasible for Heiltsuk people to make trips out into the territory, and the TUS data may help to educate young people and others about the ancestors' and elders' uses of the land and the wealth of detailed ecological knowledge that is their heritage as Heiltsuk youth. Improved access to the land stimulates curiosity

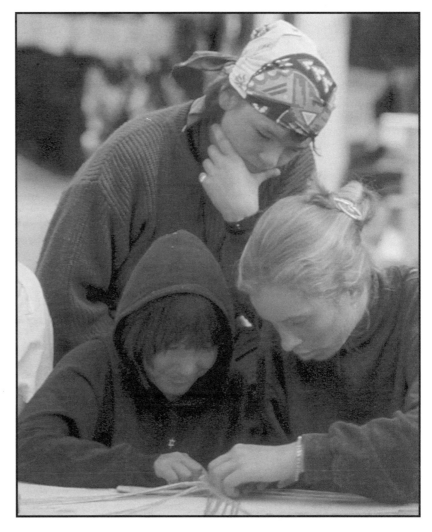

about traditional uses and traditional ecological knowledge; increased knowledge of these subjects increases the allure of trips out into the territory.

The Heiltsuk Cultural Landscape Assessment has already succeeded in building capacity and providing tools to respond to the demands of treaty negotiations, and beyond. It is also providing the framework for a vision of a conservation economy for Heiltsuk territory. It does not promise a magical flourish by which all the woes of the Heiltsuk people are laid to rest and the culture, economy and environment of the central coast suddenly achieve perfect harmony. It does, however, promise a level of awareness and an ability to act that will alter the balance of

Cultural Rediscovery camps stimulate the curiosity of youth and involve them in their traditional culture. Haisla Rediscovery camp. MYRON KOZAK opportunities back to the Heiltsuk's favour, and in favour of stewardship of the environment, a vibrant economy, and respect for indigenous culture.

There will be setbacks, no doubt, and there will be small victories, and large ones. Perhaps the Heiltsuk will settle a treaty, perhaps not. Maybe the liquidation of cedar in the territory will be stopped. Perhaps investment dollars can be deployed in the community in a way that builds assets for the Heiltsuk, rather than for everyone else. Maybe those boats bobbing at the docks will once again head out to fish, and even tourists might prove to be more of a boon than a bother.

What is certain is that external pressures on the Heiltsuk people and the resources of their territory will not go away. The economics of life in a remote coastal community will remain difficult. Developing the skills and capacity to deal effectively with these pressures and problems will be a perennial challenge. However, by integrating cultural values with economic development and conservation, the Heiltsuk are improving social and economic conditions in their community, and establishing themselves as the leaders in planning for conservation and sustainable use of resources in the territory they have always called home and always will. Theirs has been, and will again be, a conservation economy.

Fishing boats in Bella Bella harbour.
ECOTRUST CANADA

"The Government have not bought any land from us so far as we know," said Chief Bob Anderson almost a century ago, "and we are simply lending this land to the Government. We own it all. We will never change our minds in that respect, and after we are dead, our children will still hold onto the same ideas. It does not matter how long the Government takes to determine this question, we will remain the same in our ideas about this matter."

Chief Bob Anderson has long since passed away. But his children, and theirs, remain the same in their ideas about this matter.

References

B.C. Ministry of Forests. June 1999. "Mid-Coast Timber Supply Areas Analysis Report."

Heiltsuk Treaty Office and Ecotrust Canada. December, 1998. "Cooperative Working Agreement Between Heiltsuk Treaty Office On Behalf of the Heiltsuk Tribal Council & Ecotrust Canada."

Heiltsuk Tribal Council, Integrated Planning Unit. September, 2000. "Heiltsuk Integrated Marine and Land Use Plan Draft."

Scientific Panel for Sustainable Forest Practices in Clayoquot Sound. April 1995. "Sustainable Ecosystem management in Clayoquot Sound – Planning and Practices."

Tobias, T. 2000. *Chief Kerry's Moose.* Vancouver: Union of B.C. Indian Chiefs and Ecotrust Canada.

January 17 2001. *Vancouver Sun.*

MAP 5.1 Past and future logging in Heiltsuk Territory

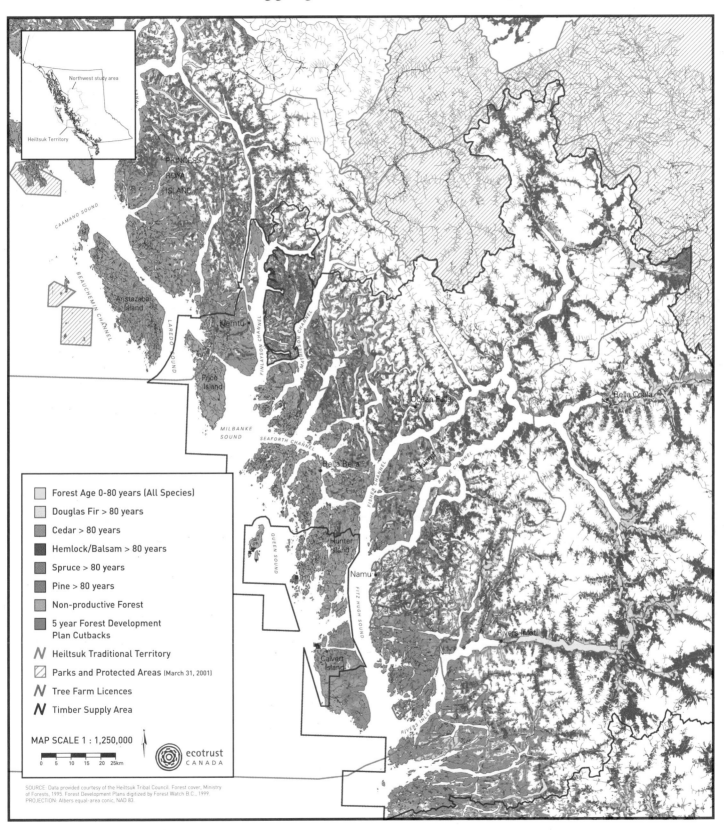

Legend:
- Forest Age 0-80 years (All Species)
- Douglas Fir > 80 years
- Cedar > 80 years
- Hemlock/Balsam > 80 years
- Spruce > 80 years
- Pine > 80 years
- Non-productive Forest
- 5 year Forest Development Plan Cutbacks
- Heiltsuk Traditional Territory
- Parks and Protected Areas (March 31, 2001)
- Tree Farm Licences
- Timber Supply Area

MAP SCALE 1 : 1,250,000

0 5 10 15 20 25km

ecotrust
CANADA

Northwest study area

Heiltsuk Territory

PRINCESS ROYAL ISLAND

CAAMANO SOUND

BEAUCHEMIN CHANNEL

Aristazabal Island

Klemtu

LAREDO SOUND

FINLAYSON CHANNEL

MATHIESON CHANNEL

Price Island

MILBANKE SOUND

SEAFORTH CHANNEL

Bella Bella

Ocean Falls

Bella Coola

BURKE CHANNEL

FISHER CHANNEL

QUEEN SOUND

Hunter Island

Namu

FITZ HUGH SOUND

Calvert Island

Rivers Inlet

RIVERS INLET

SOURCE: Data provided courtesy of the Heiltsuk Tribal Council. Forest cover, Ministry of Forests, 1995. Forest Development Plans digitized by Forest Watch B.C., 1999. PROJECTION: Albers equal-area conic, NAD 83.

A thousand-year plan

By Ian Gill

AT A-GOY-U-WA ONE STILL NIGHT BACK IN 1995, A GROUP OF PEOPLE SAT IN A CIRCLE AROUND what is known as a council fire. Besides the crackle of the fire, the only sound was of one voice. According to tradition, at a council fire the only person who is allowed to speak is whoever is holding an eagle's feather. This feather is passed from person to person – elder to child, man to woman, native to non-native – and whoever holds the feather holds the floor, so to speak. Some nights people have a lot to say, and some nights they don't. Sometimes the council fire goes to the wee hours of the morning, and other times it is a quick affair.

People often take the feather from their neighbour, stroke it for a time, and pass it along without saying anything. Other people grip the feather and talk for a very long time. Sometimes they share observations from a day just spent on Kitlope Lake, on the river, in the forest, or on the beach at A-goy-u-wa. Some impart spiritual discoveries, or share the residue of pain left over from residential schools or decades of environmental abuse in their territories. Many of the messages at a council fire are complicated, and some of them simple.

This particular night, I was fairly new to my role at Ecotrust Canada. The Kitlope, or Huchsduwachsdu Nuyem Jees as it is properly known, had recently been protected by agreement of the Haisla Nation, Ecotrust, the B.C. government and West Fraser Timber Company. A-goy-u-wa is at the heart of the Kitlope, and is perhaps its spiritual centre. It is here that, for years, elders and young people had gathered in camps run by the Haisla Nation Rediscovery Society, and literally rediscovered their connection to The Land of Milky Blue Waters.

Fresh to my role and my relationship with the Haisla – and custodian of a treasured relationship between the Haisla and Ecotrust in the U.S. which dated back to

The Kitlope Valley, the traditional territory of the Haisla Nation, has been protected from industrial resource extraction since 1994. DYLAN SIMONDS the very origin of Ecotrust – I was keen to follow through on the many good ideas that had emerged during the quiet campaign to protect Huchduwaschdu Nuyem Jees. One proposal had been to quickly establish ecotourism operations in the new protected area. So when it came my turn to speak, when I held the feather, I talked about what an enlightening day I had spent among the Haisla, and how I was eager to follow through on commitments to bring ecotours to the Kitlope as promised in a five-year plan I had read somewhere.

As befits a solemn occasion bound by protocols, no-one interrupted me. I said my piece and passed the feather. About 180 degrees later, a Haisla elder spoke. Gently, he admonished me on two counts. "Why is everyone so eager to bring development to the Kitlope? We've just spent years trying to keep development out!" And what was all this talk of a five-year plan? "We've just started work on a 1,000-year plan," he said. Of course, I wanted to jump in and qualify what I'd said, but the feather went to the next person and never came back to me. Being denied an opportunity to argue and rationalize what I had said made what he had said all the more powerful, and lasting.

We quickly found in researching this book that the conservation economy is within reach, North of Caution, and south of it too

On another night, three years later and hundreds of kilometres farther south in the coastal temperate rain forest bioregion, another elder spoke at the end of a long day during which many of us at Ecotrust had struggled through a design charette for the Jean Vollum Natural Capital Center, Ecotrust's headquarters in Portland. We had been wrestling with how to take a 100-year-old brick and beam warehouse and convert it, using green technologies and the latest design concepts, into a living example of our vision of a conservation economy.

This night, Stewart Brand spoke to a group of us over dinner, and urged that we do as little as possible to a building that, he pointed out, had done a very good job of serving its singular purpose for 100 years. He urged us to be prudent, conservative, distrustful of the latest trends and mindful that, another 100 years hence, the Natural Capital Center might be called upon to perform yet new functions that we could not even dream of. Our greatest achievement, he said, would be to restore the old warehouse without compromising its ability to be, 100 years from now, perhaps a warehouse again, or who knows what? That night, Stewart Brand talked of "the long now," and of a clock conceived by legendary computer scientist Daniel Hillis. In 1993, Hillis wrote:

"When I was a child, people used to talk about what would happen by the year 2000. Now, thirty years later, they still talk about what will happen by the year 2000. The future has been shrinking by one year per year for my entire life. I think it is time for us to start a long-term project that gets people thinking past the mental barrier of the Millennium. I would like to propose a large (think Stonehenge) mechanical clock, powered by seasonal temperature changes. It ticks once a year, bongs once a century, and the cuckoo comes out every millennium."

At Ecotrust Canada, we salute the cuckoo, who recently ushered in another millennium. And we salute our elders, near and far, who have counselled patience in a world that rewards pace, and who have urged us to have faith in people where others place faith in institutions.

When the Kitlope was protected in 1994, it was Ecotrust's ardent hope that what happened there – a powerful and unique partnership between a conservation group and a coastal First Nation – would have an immediate ripple effect all along the coast. We set out to publish a book about the northwest coast of B.C. in the hope that we might encourage a transformation of an insatiable industrial economy into a careful, conservation economy. We put the publication of such a book high among the priorities in a succession of annual plans, which years happily ticked by as we repeatedly failed to produce this book as demanded by our annual plans.

We would like to think that our patience has been rewarded with a book that will have lasting value for communities and conservation entrepreneurs who are struggling to bring the conservation economy into being. For Ecotrust Canada, this is an important book, not because we finally got something published, but because this book celebrates partnerships with the Heiltsuk and Haisla Nations, and others, that have taught us a great deal and enriched our lives immensely.

The fact is, we quickly found in researching this book that the conservation economy is within reach, North of Caution, and south of it too. The odds are still stacked heavily against those building the conservation economy, and there is still much to despair when it comes to lousy logging practices, over-fishing, tainted planning processes and the tyranny of information barriers and distortions. But these were the hallmarks of the industrial century just past, and their potency is waning.

We look ahead instead to the conservation century, the century just begun. In this century, people like the Heiltsuk and the Haisla and their neighbours all up and down the coast – native and non-native – will celebrate a return to stewardship principles that will restore and protect their territories, and restore and protect their dignity as people. On April 4, 2001, that task was made easier by an extraordinary announcement by coastal First Nations, conservationists, industry, and the provincial government that presages dramatic reductions in timber harvest levels, and an increasing say by First Nations in how their resources are developed, and by whom.

At Ecotrust, our work will continue to be centred on what we call the "just transition" of ownership of natural assets back to the indigenous communities of the B.C. coast. For communities along the coast to truly prosper, joint-ventures and side deals where large corporate interests continue to hold all the real assets will not suffice to bring about a conservation economy. Communities are entitled to own assets and access to their lands and waters, not to have them encumbered by tenures and allocations that ignore Aboriginal rights and title. So we will work with communities that seek to build and retain assets, and to find conservation-based solutions to diversifying their economies. These communities will prosper from their knowledge of their lands and waters, because it is knowledge, not muscle or machines, that will power the conservation century.

To that end, we offer this modest contribution to knowledge about places that we and our many partners hold dear. And we offer this confession: for all the wise teachings of our elders, we are desperately impatient for profound changes to take place in our existing economy, such that even five-year time horizons seem too long to us. How to work on the failures of the real now, while respecting the "long now" of one-thousand year plans is a tension in our lives that may never be resolved. Thus we urgently aid the emergence of a conservation economy. None of us will be around to hear the next bong of the millennium clock, let alone salute the next cuckoo, but there is every hope we will witness the flourishing of a conservation economy, North of Caution and beyond.

REFERENCES

http://www.longnow.org/about/about.htm

AUTHOR BIOGRAPHIES

David Carruthers

David Carruthers lives with his wife Naomi Snieckus in Vancouver. In his work, David has committed to improving access to information in the province and supporting communities with the tools required for local decision making. As Director of Information Services with Ecotrust Canada, David has contributed to many information products and publications and has built regional networks in the public information sector, including the Aboriginal Mapping Network.

Ian Gill

Ian Gill is president of Ecotrust Canada (Vancouver, B.C.) and a director of Ecotrust (Portland, Ore.), related non-profit organizations that promote the emergence of a conservation economy in the coastal temperate rain forests of North America.

Prior to founding Ecotrust Canada in November 1994, Ian was a writer-broadcaster with the Canadian Broadcasting Corporation. In his seven years as a television reporter with the CBC, Ian specialized in land-use, environment and resource issues. His television documentaries won numerous local and international awards. Ian also spent seven years as a senior reporter and editor with *The Vancouver Sun*. He is a fellow of Journalistes en Europe (1986-87).

Ian is a member of the advisory boards of the *Cascadia Times* newspaper; the Forestry Advisory Council at the University of B.C.; Douglas & McIntyre's *The Illustrated History of British Columbia;* and the Canadian Electricity Association's public advisory panel on Environmental Commitment and Responsibility.

He is the author of the best-selling *Hiking on the Edge: Canada's West Coast Trail*, and *Haida Gwaii: Journeys Through the Queen Charlotte Islands*, a finalist for the 1998 Bill Duthie Memorial Award. Ian lives in Vancouver with his partner Jennifer and their three children, Jasper, Fergus, and Lucy.

Terry Glavin

Terry Glavin is a West coast journalist, conservationist and author. The editor of *Transmontanus Books*, Glavin is a columnist for the *Georgia Straight* magazine and a frequent contributor to magazines such as *Outdoor Canada* and *Canadian Geographic*. A founding member of the Pacific Fisheries Resource Conservation Council, Glavin's most recent books include *The Last Great Sea: A Voyage Through the Human and Natural History of the North Pacific Ocean* (2000); *A Voice Great Within Us*, (1998); and *This Ragged Place: Travels Across the Landscape* (1996).

Doug Hopwood

Doug Hopwood began his forestry career operating a small-scale logging and portable sawmill business. Since studying forestry, he has worked as a consultant and instructor in forest ecology and management, timber supply analysis, biodiversity conservation, sustainability, ecosystem management, and community forestry. Doug is a Registered Professional Forester and has a B.Sc. in Forest Science from the University of British Columbia. His home on Lasqueti Island is powered by solar and micro-hydroelectric power. He rides a bicycle or takes the bus as much as possible.

Richard Manning

Author of six books including: *Food's Frontier*, a profile of nine post-Green-Revolution agricultural projects in Latin America, Asia and Africa. North Point, October, 2000. *Inside Passage*, an account of biodiversity and economy in the coastal temperate rainforests of North America. Island Press, November, 2000. *One Round River: The Curse of Gold and the Fight for the Big Blackfoot*, Henry Holt, 1998. Grassland: *The History, Biology, Politics and Promise of the American Prairie*, Viking, 1995. *A Good House: Building a Life on the Land*, Grove, 1993. *Last Stand: Logging, Journalism and the Case for Humility*, Peregrine-Smith, 1991.

Freelance magazine writer, with essays and articles published in *Harper's, The Los Angeles Times, Frankfurter Allgemeine Zeitung, The New York Times, Audubon, Outside, E Magazine, High Country News* and *Northern Lights.* Newspaper editor and reporter for fifteen years, working at newspapers in Montana and southern Idaho. Winner of the Mansfield Center's Lud Browman award for science writing, Richard Margolis award for environmental writing, Montana Audubon Society award for environmental reporting, Montana Wilderness Association award for writing, three-time winner of C.B. Blethen Award for investigative journalism. John S. Knight fellow in journalism at Stanford University in 1994-95. University of Michigan and University of Montana, political science. Lives in Lolo, Montana.

Ben Parfitt

Ben Parfitt lives in Victoria. He is a longtime writer on forestry issues. He began writing on natural resources and the conflicting visions over their use while as a reporter at *The Vancouver Sun.* He has worked as a freelance writer and consultant since 1993. He is a regular contributor to *The Georgia Straight* magazine and also writes for *Beautiful B.C.* and *B.C. Business* magazines. He is the author of *Forest Follies: Adventures and Misadventures in the Great Canadian Forest* and co-author with Michael M'Gonigle of *Forestopia: A Practical Guide to the New Forest Economy.*

Alex Rose

Alex Rose is a freelance magazine writer and author of *Spirit Dance at Meziadin: Joseph Gosnell and the Nisga'a Treaty,* published by Harbour Press in April, 2001. He also wrote *Nisga'a: People of the Nass River,* published by Douglas & McIntyre, which won the 1993 Roderick Haig-Brown British Columbia Book Prize.

Pauline Waterfall

Hilistis is the Heiltsuk ancestral name that Pauline inherited from her parental grandmother. It refers to "coming full circle with the completion of what was started" and relates to an origin story of the territory where her parental ancestors came from. This name is befitting of the community work that her grandparents challenged her to undertake. In 1944, she was born and raised in Bella Bella at a time when "modern conveniences" were unheard of and subsistence life was the norm. From an early age, she received traditional teachings and experienced the remnants of a once-vibrant culture. As a displaced youth, she was motivated to learn about her cultural roots through many Heiltsuk teachers. They helped her understand about Heiltsuk history and challenges and their teachings became personal tools of healing, recovery and empowerment. In 1990, she graduated from UBC with a teaching degree and since then her life's work has been predominately in the field of adult education. Currently, Pauline serves as the Executive Director of the Heiltsuk College, which she helped to establish.

Pauline is blessed with a large extended family. Her husband, three adult children, two granddaughters and immediate family form a strong foundation upon which she draws her strength, focus and inspiration. She continues to make important contributions to her community and is a powerful advocate and role model for her students at Heiltsuk College. As a cultural authority, Pauline's wisdom is regularly sought by those active in perpetuating Heiltsuk traditions through such ceremonies as the potlatch.

ACKNOWLEDGEMENTS

The preparation of this book was aided immeasurably by numerous individuals. We would like to acknowledge the following people and groups for their support over the years.

First, sincere thanks to the many people who were interviewed for the book. They donated their time to each of the authors and their stories gave the book its substance and voice.

We would like to acknowledge the Heiltsuk, the Tsimshian, the Haisla, the Kitasoo-Xaisxais, the Owekeeno, the Kwakiutl and the Nuxalk First Nations, for sharing their history and culture with us.

Primary editors Ian Gill and Nina Winham.

Research for *North of Caution* took place between 1996-2001. Special thanks to Erin Kellogg, Katrina Kucey, Rita Fromholt, Mike Morrell, Wendy Manchur and Melanie Mena.

Original mapping and cartographic work was coordinated by David Carruthers, with team leaders Kira Gerwing, Leah McMillin, Ian Scott, and Mike Mertens, and support by Kirsti Medig, Dorie Brownell, Tim Wilson, Steve Young, Scott Sharp, Matt Dunstan, Jamie Bonham, Patricia Jarrett, Clint Johnson and Jo-Anne Stacey.

Design and layout by Catherine Jordan of Sage Design.

We would like to thank Gary Fiegehen, Dave Nunuk, B.C. Archives, Joe Scott, Richard Manning, Alex Rose, Terry Lalonde, Len Frazer, Signy Fredrickson, Doug Hopwood, Seth Zuckerman, Cindy Hazenboom, Mike Jacobs, Kira Gerwing, Ian McAllister, Wendy Manchur, Roman Skotnicki, and Ecotrust for the use of their images. Many people appeared in photos throughout the book and we would like to thank them for their permission to reprint these photos.

Thank you to the distributor, Greystone Books, in particular Rob Sanders.

This book was made possible by the generosity of Ecotrust Canada's donors, particularly through projects grants from the C.S. Mott Foundation, David and Lucile Packard Foundation, and the Rockefeller Brothers Fund. The following donors provided general support for our work during the years the book was in production: W. Alton Jones Foundation, Bullitt Foundation, Chawkers Foundation, Compton Foundation, Donner Canadian Foundation, EJLB Foundation, Endswell Foundation, William and Flora Hewlett Foundation, Kahanoff Foundation, Henry P. Kendall Foundation, McLean Foundation, Giles W. & Elise G. Mead Foundation, George Cedric Metcalf Charitable Foundation, Moore Family Foundation, Oak Foundation, Patagonia, Turner Foundation, Weeden Foundation, and Wilburforce Foundation.